DIMENSIONAL JOURNEY

ENCOUNTERS AND TEACHINGS

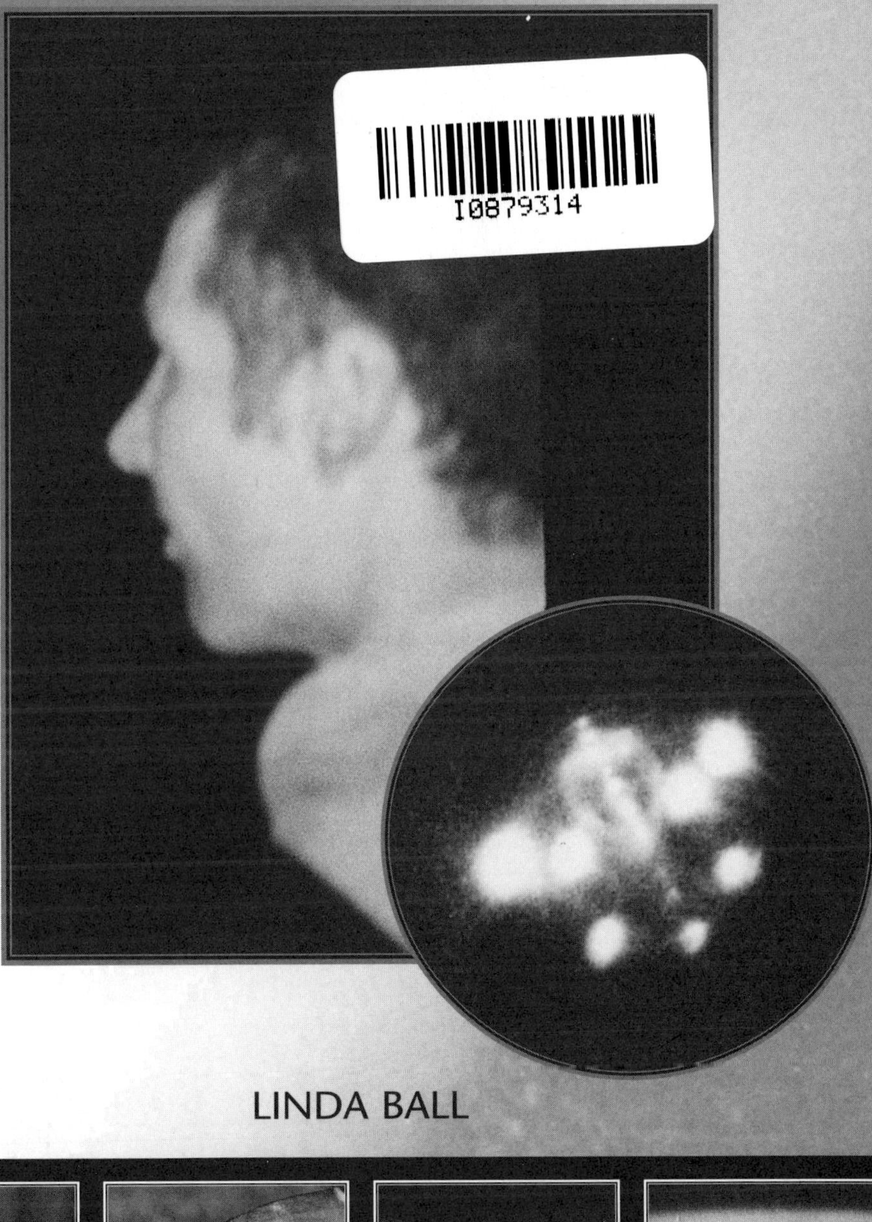

LINDA BALL

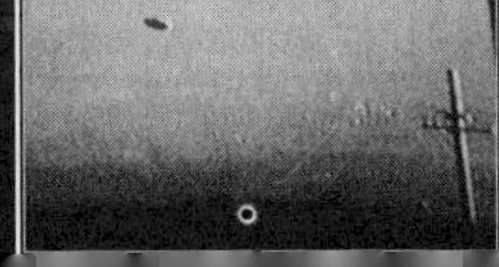

DIMENSIONAL JOURNEY
ENCOUNTERS AND TEACHINGS

by
Linda Ball

LIGHT Technology
PUBLISHING

ISBN 1-891-824-34-1

Published by

Light Technology Publishing
P.O. Box 3540
Flagstaff, AZ 86003
1-800-450-0985
e-mail: publishing@lighttechnology.com
www.lighttechnology.com

Printed by

GraphTech
DIGITAL & PRINTING

CONTENTS

Yes, our one, shall we talk of this title a bit more? The word, dimensional, gives the premise that there is more than one dimension to something. When that word is used in conjunction with journey, it implies there have been what one might perceive as multiple dimensions of that journey.

Let us look at the multiple dimensions of your journey thus far. Firstly, there was the discovery of the dimensions within yourself: subconscious, conscious and super-conscious. These all share the same space-time continuum within you as an existent being. Secondly, through your experiences along your path of enlightenment you have had many variations of discovery. The elementary lessons and experiences were given to the toddler that you were in the beginning. As your awareness heightened, more levels of knowledge were brought forth to accommodate your level, or dimension, of comprehension. Layers upon layers of keys have opened doors of awareness, giving access to the discovery of who, in truth, you are. Thusly, dimensional journey. All of these dimensions remain in the space-time continuum of you.

Do you remain the toddler who first stepped upon this path? No, of certainty you are not. This realization could be seen as a parallel to the message on Generations. This being, known as Linda, has emerged into a far more mature entity in relation to spiritual awareness. This journey is not completed and, as you go forth, you might find yourself "slipping" into more dimensions of the discovery of you.

Montana, February 2002

ACKNOWLEDGMENTS

I wish to give thanks and acknowledgment to the two people who were most influential in the accomplishment of this book. To my husband, Dennis, who stood beside me through thick and thin. His continual support and encouragement were a great catalyst in the completion of *Dimensional Journey*. His faith in me is a gift beyond measure.

I also want to thank my publisher, O'Ryin Swanson. Through her open willingness and confidence in me, this message has come to fruition.

LIST OF PHOTOS

Photographer: © Linda Ball.

TOM (DONGO) HAD ASKED ME TO PHOTOGRAPH HIM AS HE MEDITATED, ENVISIONING AN ORB OF LIGHT. THE ORB DID APPEAR.

INTRODUCTION

In the following pages I share a story that might appear to some as incredible, and yet it is true. We all reach a junction on the path of our awakening that is a turning point. Events, circumstances or perhaps unexplainable experiences are often the catalysts that propel us onto a journey of discovery, which then provides the keys to the answers we seek. Our questions are manifold, but there is often a common thread that runs through them: What exists beyond the boundaries of this existence I am experiencing? Inwardly our heart whispers to us that there is more. I heard the whispers of my heart often, and yet I could not pull forth or envision what they were softly telling me. In time the once soft whispers became louder and began to shout at my consciousness. It was then that I chose to awaken, and I found myself engulfed in the greatest mystery one could imagine.

Anomalous events began after my move to the Bradshaw Ranch in the beautiful and mystical area of Sedona, Arizona. In a previous book entitled *Merging Dimensions*, which I cowrote under the name of Linda Bradshaw, I relayed some of the events that stretched the parameters of my beliefs to the maximum. I again share some of these occurrences, and more.

My perception of reality was tested and questioned again and again as I had encounters with extraterrestrials, Bigfoot and other humanlike entities that towered over me. I was able to photograph much of the phenomena, which began rather benignly with wafting, multi-colored orbs of light, then escalated over seven years to the more heart-stopping episodes where I encountered and interacted with otherworldly beings. Each encounter was different, making it necessary for me to go within to discern, or detect, the intent of these beings. I needed to be on high alert at all times. One experience might cause my stomach to churn, while another would leave me breathless and tingling from an angelic presence. There was no specific time frame in which to predict these happenings. Perhaps one to two weeks would go by with no evidence of my visitors, then there would be nightly occurrences. Why was this happening? I asked myself time and again.

Often I would review my life, in an effort to perhaps find a starting point or cause for these bizarre experiences I was now living. Since my life began quite normally, having been raised by loving parents in a very normal home and atmosphere, I could not find an explanation using this approach. Were these phenomena perhaps exclusive of the ranch? Was I merely catapulted into this Galactic Park, as my son had dubbed the ranch, by "accident"? In reality though, there are no "accidents."

Over time I came to realize that my experiences on Bradshaw Ranch were monumental to my growth and awareness. This became even more apparent through channeled messages that I had started receiving in 1985, several years prior to my residence on the ranch. These communications, filled with love and wisdom, sustained me through some difficult times, and as my experiences on the ranch escalated, so did the messages. The incredible phenomena I experienced alone could have filled this book. However, a big piece of the puzzle would be missing if I would not have included some of the messages that I received, which have provided guidance that sustained and strengthened me. These wise words aptly apply not just to myself, but to all.

One major theme in these messages was that there was nothing to fear. My messengers taught me that first I must recognize who I truly am, who we all truly are; through this revelation of my connection to Source, then, would I understand that there was nothing in my experiences that could harm me. Fully comprehending this did not happen automatically for me, though. Often I found myself confronted with what seemed to me fearful or strange experiences. Only after many such instances and lovingly guided by my messengers did I realize that the sense of fear I felt in such encounters was but my own perception.

I no longer reside on the ranch and have relocated to northwestern Montana. One might ask if the phenomena still continue. To that I can answer unequivocally, "Yes, they do." However, they have taken on another form. As we each grow and learn, events and experiences also change to accommodate each stage of our trek here on Earth. The messages have never stopped, and I continue to be nourished by them. What treasures they hold and how selfish I would be to forever hoard them for my growth alone. Divine knowledge belongs to no one individual, for we are all *one.*

Lest one should think that I am "special" or more highly gifted than others, I wish to assure you that this is not the case. We are all equal, and the only difference is one's personal perception of oneself. My messengers taught me this so eloquently as I endured each rut and bump along my path. I invite you to join me on my multidimensional journey throughout the following pages and meet some of the beings who assisted me in a great revelation.

[illegible]

AUTHOR'S NOTE

God is portrayed often in the following messages, and the identity, God, is referred to as being of the male gender. This was done to simplify the messages, with the understanding that I was aware of the true gender of the Creator. To that extent, earlier messages had explained to me that God is neither male nor female. God is the culmination of both genders, thusly being He/She. God is an essence from which we evolve. By the same token, mankind (male and female) is often referred to as man.

I pray that the messages bring healing, awareness and enlightenment to those who read these words.

—Linda L. Ball

SECTION I

AT THE RANCH

Photographer: © Linda Ball.

FAST-MOVING ENERGY BETWEEN THE HOUSE AND TREE.

▲ SOME LIGHT ANOMALIES ZIPPED BY AT INCREDIBLY FAST SPEEDS.

▼ OTHERS HOVERED, FLOATING SEVERAL FEET ABOVE THE GROUND.

Photographer: © Linda Ball.

HOVERING ORB BY THE RANCH HOUSE.

The Bradshaw Ranch was an incredibly beautiful place near Sedona, Arizona. We often referred to it as Galactic Park, after my son, Victor, humorously had so defined the area. The new name aptly described that enigmatic wonderland. The encounters I was privileged to experience there took me on a journey like none other. As in all life, some of the experiences were somewhat traumatic, whereas others took me to glorious heights of which I'd never known.

Bradshaw Ranch was very secluded, an "island" of private property that was completely surrounded by Forest Service land. There were no visible neighbors; the closest one lived about two miles away. The ranch was located twelve miles from town, and for eight of these miles we had to navigate a rough, bumpy road to get home. The property consisted of ninety acres of high-desert terrain, abundant with both cedar and juniper trees and open spaces that were covered with grasses and shrubs. An unoccupied residence was at the north end of the property; at the east side, set several yards apart, were the newer house where we resided as well as an old adobe homestead, built in 1902. There were also several corrals and a Western movie town, where a fair number of movies had been filmed. Bradshaw Ranch had quite a movie history, but before long, it was also to be known as a high-activity area of phenomena.

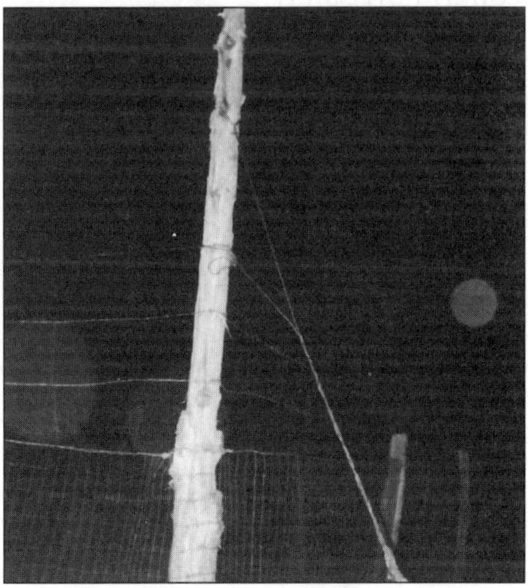

Photographer: © Linda Ball.

Orb of light hovering by a fence.

When I first set foot on the ranch, I was struck by its beauty. This quiet, pristine place was nestled in a valley surrounded by rolling hills and majestic red rock formations that jutted loftily skyward. The land exuded an incredible peace and gave me the feeling that I had been transported to another place, and yet I was still here on Earth.

However, nighttime soon started bringing the feeling of a "presence" that I could not completely discern, yet intuitively I would be put on alert. At times sounds filtered in, and our dogs would frantically bark their protests at intruders. Other times these same dogs would cower in a corner and whimper. What had happened? Who or what was there? Over time these visits were no longer exclusive to the dark hours of the night. Rather, I began to feel the by then all-too-familiar presences also in the daylight hours, altering the feeling of the ranch. Some visitors would intensify the incredible peace we had become so accustomed to; others would disrupt the harmony of the land.

Initially, I thought that I was the only person who was having these experiences and encounters. Had I become delusional? Thankfully, this was not the case. In time, others also encountered the strange visitors, and I soon discovered that I could photograph the anomalous energies and beings that came to visit and thusly confirm my sanity.

CHAPTER ONE

LIGHTS

The phenomena began with orbs of light that appeared to be wafting in close proximity as I walked the property at night. I was quite intrigued when I first became aware of these orbs. Initially, I could not see them with my eyes; rather, I could intuitively sense an energy about me, indicating that "something" was nearby. I began pointing my camera at this energy, and the photos I took showed beautiful orbs of light. In time, my eyes adjusted, and I occasionally caught a glimpse of the orbs' beauty as they hovered nearby. The colors were fascinating and displayed a spectrum of hues ranging from white, pink, pale red and orange to blue and various shades in between. Their sizes also varied.

One of the things I immediately noticed about these orbs of light was that they emitted a sense of peace and tranquillity whenever they were in close proximity. Occasionally they would, in a sense, attach themselves to not only me, but also to others as our curiosity pushed us forward, trying to discover just what or who they were.

Some of these light anomalies would hover, floating several feet

LIGHT ANOMALIES WITH BROKEN OR SCALLOPED PERIMETERS.

FAST-MOVING LIGHT ENERGY ZIPPING EITHER AWAY FROM OR TOWARD THE HOUSE.

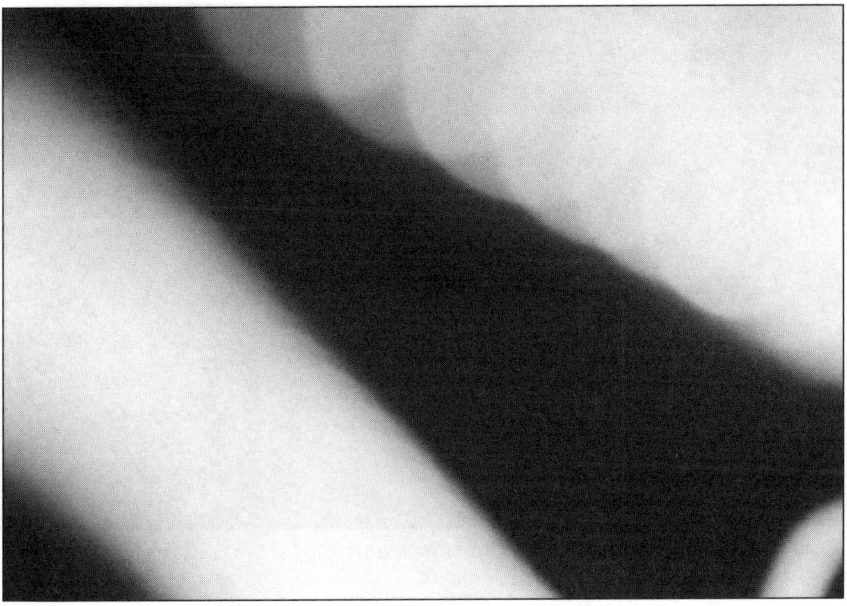

Photographer: © Linda Ball.

CLOSE-UP OF FAST-MOVING ORBS.

HERE ARE SOME EXAMPLES OF THE MANY DIFFERENT TYPES OF ORBS. THIS AND THE FOLLOWING PAGE SHOW HOW DIFFERENT THE ORBS OF LIGHT I EXPERIENCED ON BRADSHAW RANCH WERE.

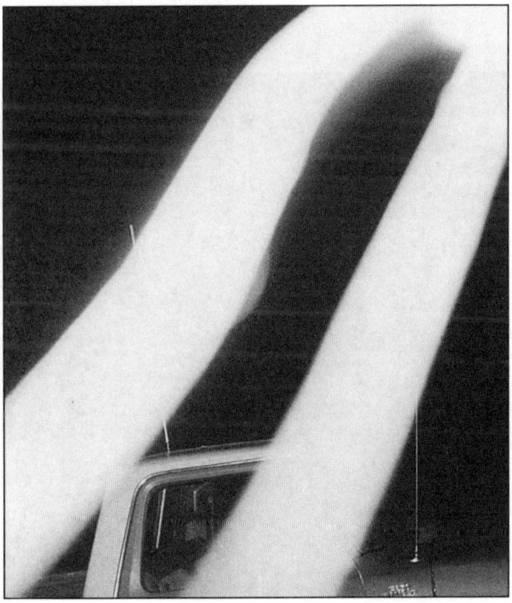

Photographer: © Linda Ball.

FAST ORB MOVING UPWARDS, PAST VICTOR'S TRUCK.

Photographer: © Linda Ball.

ORBS OF LIGHT WITH TRUCK; TOM DONGO IN THE FRONT AND JIM SWEEL IN THE BACKGROUND.

THE COLORS OF THE LIGHT ORBS RANGED FROM WHITE, PINK, A PALE RED AND ORANGE TO BLUE AND VARIOUS SHADES IN BETWEEN. THEY EMITTED A SENSE OF PEACE AND TRANQUILLITY WHENEVER THEY WERE IN CLOSE PROXIMITY.

Photographer: © Linda Ball.

MULTI-COLORED ORBS OF LIGHT.

above the ground. They appeared to be stationary or moved slowly in a particular area. Other, smaller orbs, which projected a more intense energy, could be caught zipping by at an incredibly fast speed. In spite of my close observations, it is impossible for me to categorize all the orbs of light; there simply were so many different ones.

Photographer: © Linda Ball.

ORBS OVER GROUND.

In the beginning I tried to use human logic in an attempt to explain the orbs of light. Were they perhaps balls of some sort of gas being emitted from the Earth? Intuitively I knew this was not the case and quickly dismissed that explanation. This was a life form. And as the following experience shows, my assessment proved to be correct.

On one very active evening, I went about quickly, taking one photo after another of the lights, which seemed to be everywhere. My son, Victor, was out with me, and we were doing our best to document all that was going on. He busily scanned with the camcorder while I used my camera. Out of the corner of my eye, I spotted a somewhat different ball of light glowing through a window from inside the old adobe homestead. I instantly sensed a life energy emitting from that light, and it appeared to focus on us as we wandered toward it.

I pointed my camera in the direction of the old house and clicked, but to no avail; the batteries in my camera had suddenly drained. This was not a natural occurrence, as I had just inserted new batteries that day and had not taken enough photos to deplete them. I voiced my disappointment as Victor aimed his camcorder at the culprit. He started to zoom in and—*zap!* All of a sudden, his battery was also dead, even though it had been recharged just prior to our excursion. Obviously, that particular light was camera-shy, and I realized that we would photograph only those of the strange lights that allowed us to do so.

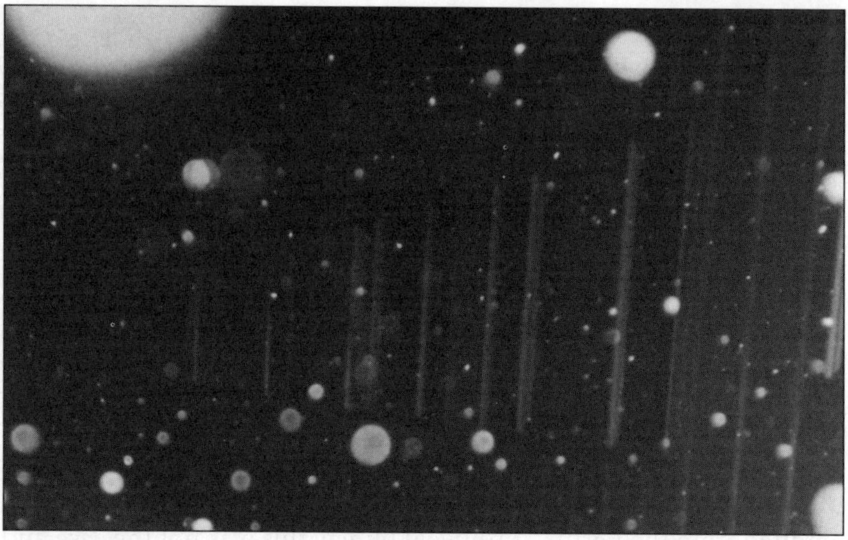

Photographer: © Linda Ball.

MULTITUDES OF ORBS BY THE RANCH HOUSE.

▲ AT TIMES THE LIGHT ORBS APPEARED IN LARGE NUMBERS. I TOOK THESE PHOTOS ON A DRY,
▼ CLEAR NIGHT.

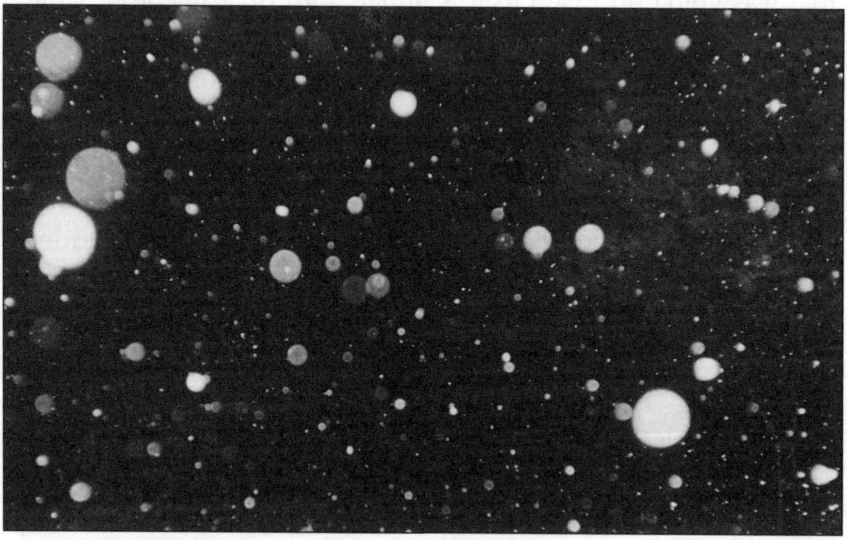

Photographer: © Linda Ball.

MULTITUDES OF ORBS OVER TREE AND FIELD.

Photographer: © Linda Ball.

STREAM OF LIGHT IN FRONT OF TREE.

THESE STREAMS OR STREAKS OF LIGHT APPEARED OFTEN, AND WITH THEM WE SENSED A MORE INTENSE ENERGY AS THEY ZIPPED PAST AT AN INCREDIBLE SPEED.

Photographer: © Linda Ball.

STREAM OF LIGHT IN FRONT OF THE OLD ADOBE HOMESTEAD.

Photographer: © Tom Dongo.

THIS FLAME WHIZZED PAST US, JUST A FEW FEET AWAY.

The Flame

The atmosphere was electrified one evening as Tom and I walked around, flashing one anomaly after another. As so often, we could see some of these energies while others remained invisible, and we could only feel them.

Tom's photo of the flame is one of the most breathtaking ones in the collection from that night. Whatever it is—the energy was intense, brilliant red with a flaming gold center. The flame had appeared just a few feet away from us, skimming above the ground as it whizzed past. If you look closely you can see the faint outline of a tree just to the right of it.

My trek to Sedona, along with the events I was privileged to experience on the Bradshaw Ranch, provided me with the focus I needed for my continual search for this elusive deity known as God. At what point in our lives do the thoughts of God become most prevalent? I had always embraced a curiosity that led me to many churches, of diverse religions and doctrines, and I had found pearls of truth that ran through each one, yet I knew something was missing. Like so many of us, I too, had to go through trauma, sadness or abnormal experiences before I could really begin my search.

God

My dearest one, there needn't be confusion. Who is God? What are the words of this supreme being? Why must one seek His origin, His will? Why indeed?

Because, my precious one, He is Source, sustenance. He is the beginning and the end. He is evermore *All That Is.* There is so much confusion and misinterpretation of His will. His will is that of love. His will is that of everything that appears before your eyes. His will *is.*

This brings us to the question, "What is life?" It is His will. His will is that His people achieve life in His light. They are not to be burdened as so many innocently misunderstand. His people are to be free in love and to love all that is. For all that is, is of God. Do you not see this? This is the hidden agenda in a great misinterpretation upon your land at this time. Many say all *is* God. No, all is *of* God. Those of stringent doctrinal beliefs state that all that is good is of God and all that is not good is of Satan. My one, please understand, *all* is of God. If God is omnipresent and omnipotent, then *everything,* even that which is called evil, had at one time emanated from God. Can we have a dichotomy? I think not. For, you see, if God is creator of all, how can there be anything that is not of this supreme being? So then how might these evil things come about?

Let us look closer. All is of God, and yet evil has arrived. Many see evil or Satan as a threat. This is powerful, yet only in one's mind. For if God is manifester of all, then He is manifester of you, and you, being of Him, have all rights of supreme power through Him. If this be true, then how might a force or faction not of Him have power over you?

Now, you might ask, "If God is power over all, then He is power over evil, and yet, like us, why would not the evil have inherent supreme power from the Lord God?" This is the ▶

mystery, my one, that ever so many refuse to solve within themselves. The evil arises not from God, but from humans. The evil is manifest out of one's neglect to see and claim one's supreme authority and heritage from God. So, you see, all that is *real* is of God. All that is *unreal* is a manifestation of oneself. Yes, this force is real because *you* gave it life. This is where you can truly understand that you, of God, are also a creator. To receive full awareness and inheritance of one's origin, one must come to this realization and then choose what one wishes to create—God or evil. I sense your reluctance at this statement, so I must explain further. When I say "create God," it must be seen as such: "create love." For God is love. Anything other than love is not of God, and it is therefore unreal, but unreality can become very real to you if you choose to create it and live in it.

Pretense is, shall we say, "fun" for a time, is it not? So, therefore, many choose to play and pretend with this area of unreality to the extent that they forget what reality is. They then find themselves bogged down in negativism and thusly surrender to the monster they have created. They are now slave to an unreal monster. Once they can see the illusion that is controlling them they might rise up and see that there is *no* power greater than that which they have through the only true and real life—and that is God. That is their home. The wheel turns and turns as multitudes struggle to free themselves. They know something is wrong, and yet they cannot see.

How sad that the words of our Father have become a bondage as humans [His creation] have attempted to place *their* bondage into the interpretation of such freeing and enlightening words. You see, the Bible is a puzzle to be solved, and only when beings allow themselves to see the light can the *true* meaning come forth. Can we not see that Satan, evil and dark forces exist because *man* has created them? Yes, ▶

your Bible tells you this, and yet many do not see. They run screaming in fear, spreading panic wherever they go, out of ignorance. May I explain further?

This text [the Bible] states that Lucifer and his angels were dismissed from the heavenly host's presence because they desired equality with the Creator. Can we not see that our attempt to *reinterpret* His words constitutes a desire of equality? Or much worse, that this could—and does—constitute a desire to override His word? Have humans chosen to see themselves in this light? I think not. For, you see, this would make them Satan, would it not? In this one exercise, humans have created this evil that they are running, screaming from. You, ones, are running from yourselves.

This be the reason, I say, to look past the pages. Be willing to hear the Lord Highest without another one's interpretation. Be open to *His* voice as *He* calls you to truth. Do not allow a severance in communication to continue this sham of belief in powerlessness over an unreal being. Again, this dark presence or being exists and has power because humanity has created it and given it power.

Yes, many will come forth with multitudes of Scripture to refute this truth, but one must remember that the misinterpretation is also being quoted. One must see that many hidden metaphors are given in these words, and upon close review it can be seen that, although darkness and evil are brought forth in this text [the Bible], humans are also shown that *they* create and give power to this in their denial of their greatness and their relationship to the God of the Highest. Think upon this strongly, and ask your Father to share with you His wisdom. He will tell you truth. He will tell you truth.

It is to my understanding that there is a great misconception of the great deity, God. For you see, He, the Source, has been disguised, misinterpreted and misdiagnosed. I use this ▶

latter term because many see our heavenly Source as somewhat of a disease. He is there, they are not quite certain where He came from, and He makes them uncomfortable. Why is this? It is due to a misconception of enormous magnitude.

Why, why, why must God make us uncomfortable? Why must He be something or someone to "contend with"? Why indeed? For, you see, in truth, He is a source to blend with. God, my one, is truth. In that form, He cannot be negative, threatening or subversive. Truth is always good in its pure form. If your perception brings Him before you as anything other than that, it is *exactly* that! *Your* perception . . .

Now, you might ask, "How can I change my perception to truth?" It is indeed very simple, but working within your present environment of life upon Earth it can also be (and usually is) difficult. Why is this? It is because the human species has insisted upon categorizing God, the Father, within the ever so limited guidelines of human comprehension. Try, my one, as you may, this can never be done. For you see, humans, in their limited spectrum of conception, cannot fathom the vastness and magnificence of this called God. How can one take the Creator and cubbyhole Him into the *creation's* idea of form or fact? This is where one's faith must emerge. For, you see, even though there are ever so many seekers, until one can move *into* the vastness of truth and *out* of human logic and perception, the truth of His being [God] can never be found. May I explain further?

There are ever so many religions formed by humans to perceive and purport their vision of God. This is just what it is . . . *their* vision. Ever so few have stepped forth through the veil and out of circumstance to see, in truth, His word and His being.

Let us say that you are Catholic, or Protestant, or Jewish, or Hindu, or Muslim, or, or, or . . . the labels of perceptions go on ▶

and on. Who, you ask, holds the key to truth? All of them and none of them. Each faction has grasped a tiny portion of truth, a pearl of wisdom, and then covered it over with layer upon layer of man's *perception* of this pearl of truth. Ultimately, there are so many layers wrapped around this gem that it is no longer visible to the human eye. How then might this truth be uncovered? Only, my one, when you are willing to set aside man's eye and replace it with a sincere desire for truth. This is God's eye, for God sees only truth. How many, I ask, scramble to and fro, seeking an answer from one faction and then another? Some become so zealous that their search becomes the focus rather than the goal of opening the God-eye within and seeing the truth that has been before them all the time. There is nothing to seek, only something to claim. I repeat this again and again.

Not all humans, certainly very few, are prepared to step out of the role of seeker, chasing elusive answers from another seeker. In your heart, do you know many who have claimed their heritage and identity? I think not. Many appear outwardly as knowledgeable, but this is merely a screen to cover the fact that they are still diligently seeking. One follows another who says, "Follow me. I am a person of God, and I can show you the way." Think again, my one. For, you see, the simple fact that they still have a need to avow and exert their "knowledge" is indeed a sign that they are still seeking. This is not wrong. It is a normal step in the progression toward home. What I state is this: A seeker will grasp another seeker, and on and on. The blind leading the blind . . .

Only those who have come to the realization that they have no need for another person to show them the way can and will step upon a new plateau where the vision is clear. It is unadulterated. It has been washed of all myths, misperceptions and ego-driven conclusions of man. You see, only man in the human form has a need to be right. Only man in the ▶

basest form has a need to control. Only humans in seeking mode will have the audacity to tell another they have all the answers. True lightbeings *know* and *experience* God within them. They cannot be ego-driven, only loving. They will stand aside as their brothers and sisters scramble to get the front seat on the bus for home. These ones, with egos rampant, shake their heads and scorn all who do not see *their* vision.

True vision, a light one knows, is only love, and in this love resides God. But do not think that seekers might instantaneously "decide" to exude love, suppressing the current logic that still resides within. This is not truth. This is another mask that merely holds one back. When they can see this clearly, they will then love, because it is the only emotion they can find. They will then experience God, because they have returned to blend with their true life source and, as one, God will be all they can see.

CHAPTER TWO

THE INVISIBLES

At times, the orbs of light did not reveal themselves to the naked eye, but I had learned to obtain pictures of them using still camera and camcorder. Thus, I was somewhat prepared when other invisibles appeared. Still, at this point I felt I was getting in over my head, so I asked Tom Dongo, a local researcher, for assistance. Tom had written several books on the phenomena in the area of Sedona, and I was hoping he could provide some further insight into the mysterious events I had experienced. He began to join me on my excursions on the ranch, and in unison, we photographed many of my invisible visitors.

The First Humanlike Being

Time and again we found that beings would walk past and almost brush our arms. We could even hear their footsteps as the grass crunched beneath their feet, but we could not see them—except at rare occasions, when they would allow us to catch a glimpse of them to help us confirm that our imaginations had not started taking over. However, we discovered that, just as with the orbs of light, we could photograph these visitors.

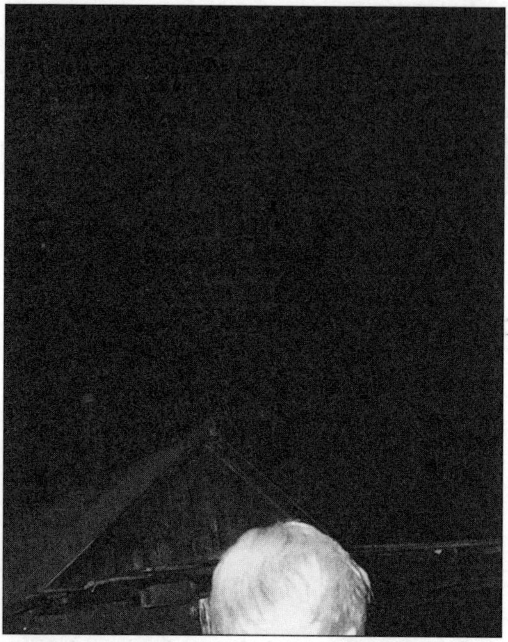

Photographer: © Tom Dongo.

TOM'S PHOTO OF THE FIRST HUMANOID BEING CAUGHT ONLY THE TOP OF THE BEING'S HEAD FROM THE FRONT, WITH HAIR FALLING SIDEWAYS OVER THE FOREHEAD.

Once again, Tom and I were out walking on the ranch, this time armed with our cameras. We were near the adobe and the main house, when all of a sudden, Tom sensed someone behind him. Quickly and without turning around, he lifted his camera above his head, aimed it at the presence and pressed the shutter release. Again without turning around, he then brought the camera to his side, directed it behind him to catch the body and pressed the shutter release. I stood quietly and watched as he captured this visitor on film.

The photos we picked up from the lab very clearly showed a being with a head and body. Because of the camera angle, Tom's first photo caught only the top of the being's head from the front, with hair falling sideways over the forehead. The second photo shows a definite body, photographed from the side, visible from the stomach down.

What was almost even more intriguing, however, was the small object hovering to the left of the being's legs. We were to this object again, next to another, totally different being we dubbed the "Blue Man."

The Blue Man

Tom and I we were out photographing. As I found myself near the especially large juniper tree that grew right by our ranch house, I sensed someone very tall standing next to me. I mentioned this to Tom, who, with his heightened perception of things not readily visible, agreed with me that this being was indeed rather tall.

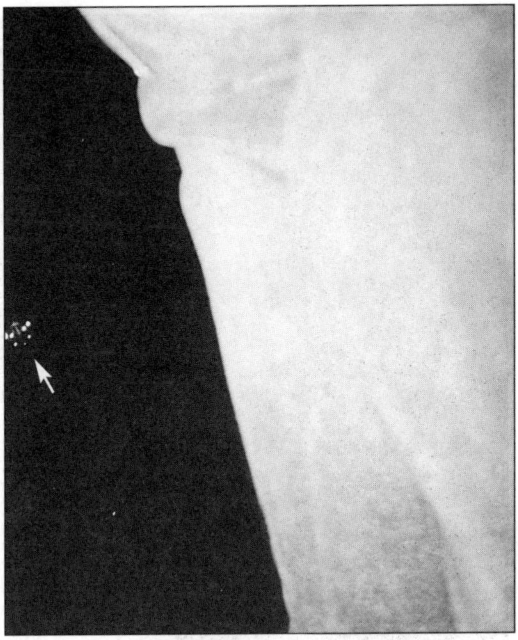

Photographer: © Tom Dongo.

THE SECOND PHOTO TOM TOOK OF THIS FIRST HUMANOID BEING SHOWS A DEFINITE BODY FROM THE STOMACH DOWN, PHOTOGRAPHED FROM THE SIDE.
THE SMALL OBJECT HOVERING BY THE BEING'S LEGS APPEARED AGAIN, NEXT TO ANOTHER, TOTALLY DIFFERENT BEING WE DUBBED THE "BLUE MAN".

I wanted to take a photo, in the hope that this being, as others before, would show up on film. Something was different this time, though; I sensed that I needed our visitor to give us permission to photograph, so I telepathically told the invisible that I was going to take a picture. Receiving approval, I turned to my right and pressed the shutter release twice, with only a couple of seconds between the shots. Knowing that the being was much taller than myself, I purposely aimed high with the first click of the shutter, then lowered my camera closer to the ground for the second one. At the same time Tom, who was standing before me, approximately ten feet away, directed his camera toward the lower torso of this person. Although we hadn't had the time to discuss how to best photograph our visitor, it worked out perfectly. The finished prints showed that each of us had photographed a different portion of the body, completing a full image.

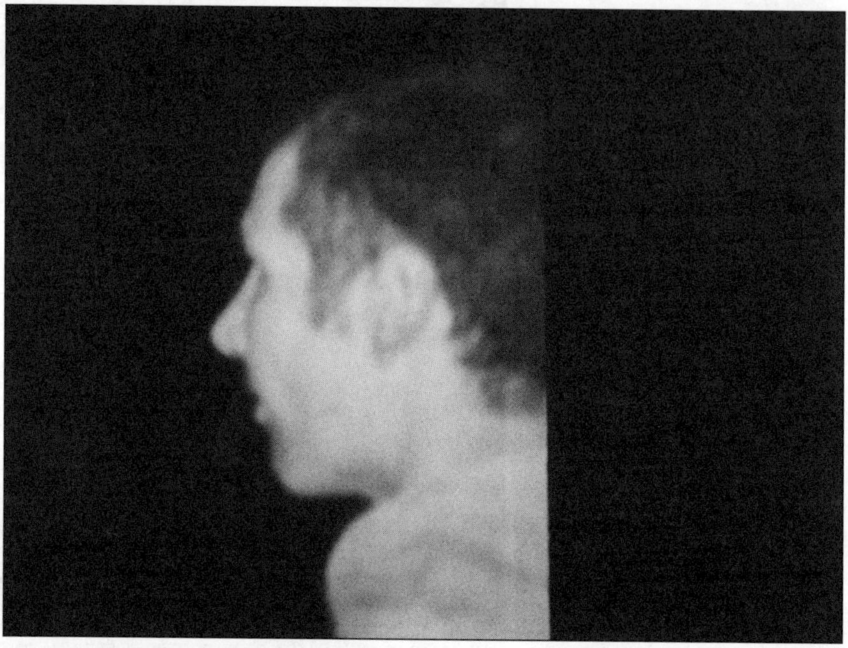

Photographer: © Linda Ball.

THE BLUE MAN'S UPPER TORSO AND HEAD.

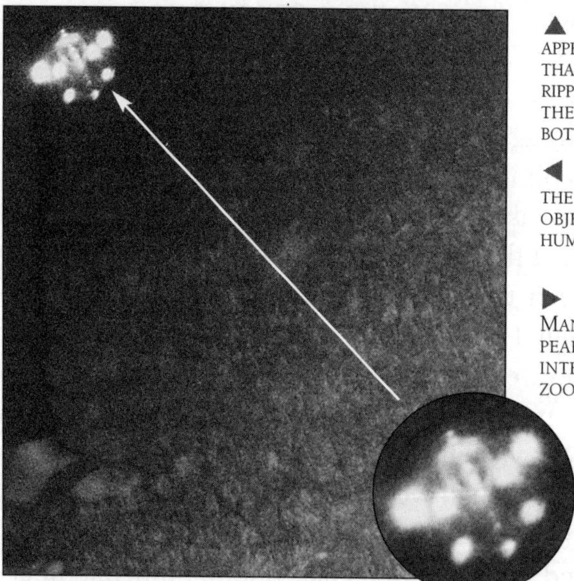

Photographer: © Tom Dongo.

THE BLUE MAN'S LEG AND FEET.

▲ THE BEING'S EAR OPENING APPEARS TO BE AT THE TOP RATHER THAN THE BOTTOM, AND THERE IS A RIPPLED RIDGE OF CARTILAGE ALONG THE OUTSIDE EDGE AND ON THE BOTTOM.

◀ NOTE THE OBJECT HOVERING BY THE BEING'S LEG. IT IS THE SAME OBJECT WE SAW BY THE FIRST HUMANLIKE BEING

▶ (OPPOSITE PAGE) THE BLUE MAN'S PHYSICAL BODY HAS DISAPPEARED. IN ITS STEAD IS AN INTENSE AMOUNT OF ENERGY ZOOMING AWAY FROM US.

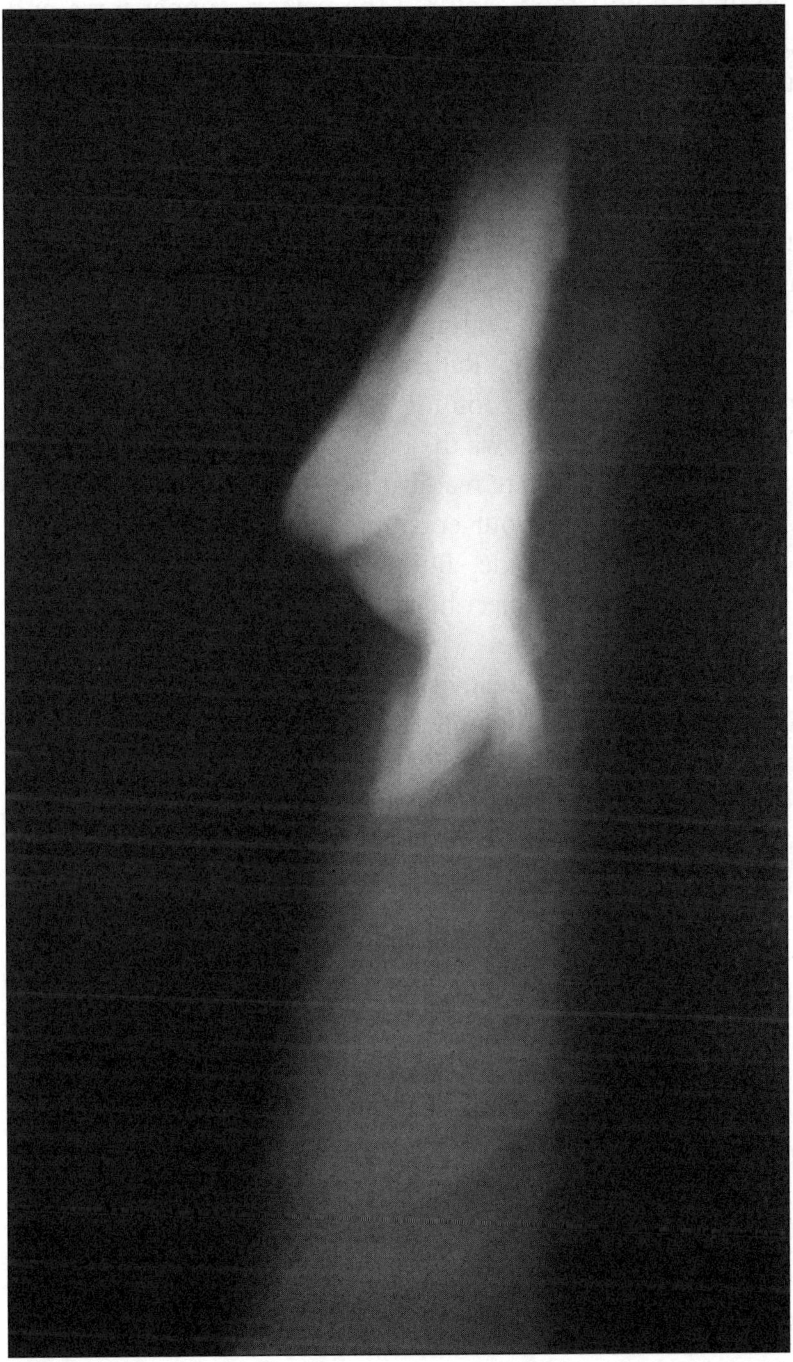

The Blue Man's physical body has disappeared, and in its stead is this quickly moving streak of light. Note the density of form within it.

Photographer: © Linda Ball.

The first photo I took captured the person's upper torso and head. A close look reveals two unusual elements about this being. Firstly, the face has a pale blue tinge to it. Inquiries at the photo lab discounted the possibility that this was caused by an overflow of color from the being's robe. Secondly, the ear is formed somewhat differently than our ears. The opening appears to be at the top rather than the bottom, and there is a rippled ridge of cartilage along the outside edge and on the bottom.

The second shot taken with my camera amazed us. No longer was there a physical body. Rather, there appeared to be only an intense amount of energy zooming away from us.

Tom's photo clearly shows the bottom half of the being.

The robe and sandals are readily discernible, and we wondered about his footwear since our encounter took place in the winter and it was quite cold outside. But there was more.

The photo shows an object hovering by the being's leg, and we had seen this object before! The same object showed up on the photo of the first humanlike invisible Tom and I encountered, hovering next to *his* leg. Although I asked several researchers who were rather knowledgeable about UFOs and other phenomena, no one could offer an explanation for this object. To this day, I do not know what it is.

Lightening the photo showed the huge juniper tree next to which I was standing during our encounter with the Blue Man. We measured the tree from the ground up to where the being's head is shown on the photograph. He was approximately eight to ten feet tall!

The Photographer

Not all phenomena happened outside our home. One type of visitation left me baffled, and to this day I still wonder about it.

I was a very frequent customer of First Light Photo Lab in Sedona. The people working there had become accustomed to the bizarre photos that appeared on the film Tom and I brought in and often looked forward to receiving more rolls of film from us. One never knew what would appear on that photographic paper. It was not uncommon for me to drop off several rolls of film at a time, since we shot hundreds of frames.

One day I stopped by the photo lab to pick up the prints from three rolls of film, all shot outside—at least I thought they were all shot outside. Scanning the finished photos, I looked in puzzlement at several before me. There were shots taken inside the house, mostly at nighttime. How strange . . . I knew I had not taken any interior shots.

When I arrived at home, I asked all who had been in the house within that week if they, perhaps, had used my camera to take some photos of the living room and kitchen. All shook the head in denial. Each of us had our own personal cameras anyhow, so it wasn't likely, that someone would need to use mine.

The photos were definitely strange. A couple of them showed the ceiling lights in the kitchen. They appeared to be turned on, glowing in an almost golden color, and yet the periphery around

Photographer: © unknown.

KITCHEN AND TREE OUTSIDE, EVERYTHING DISTORTED.

them was totally black. This made no sense. If the lights were on, the area around them would be lit as well.

Although most photos were taken in the nighttime, there was one that either appeared to have been taken during the day or a brilliant light had been coming through the kitchen window when the shot was taken. This photo showed that not only everything in the kitchen appeared to be coming apart molecularly, but also the large juniper tree outside the kitchen window. How could that be? At first I assumed the camera had been moved as the photo was being snapped, but after further scrutiny, this did not seem to be the case. What was going on? I was determined to find out.

For several evenings I slept on the living room sofa with my camera lying on the coffee table close to me. From that vantage point I had a great view not only of the living room, but also of the adjacent kitchen. It did not work; I did not get any new anonymous photos.

I consulted with Tom who suggested that I dust the camera with some powder or talc to see if any fingerprints showed up. Before retiring to the bedroom one evening, I did as Tom had suggested. I carefully dusted my camera with white powder and left it in clear

Photographer: © Linda Ball.

THE BEING WHO LEFT THE PRINTS APPEARED TO HAVE ONE VERY POINTED APPENDAGE WITH A SHORT, WIDE DIGIT NEXT TO IT.

view in the living room. The following morning there were prints, all right, but they were not human. The being who left the prints appeared to have one very pointed appendage with a short, wide digit next to it.

Photographer: © Linda Ball.

THE LEFT SIDE OF THE CAMERA.

This was just too bizarre. I desperately wanted to discover the mysterious photographer, but it did not happen, and I never received another interior mystery photograph. This was yet another incident that I added to my long list of unsolved mysteries.

Pigs?!

The morning after a particularly eventful night brought us invisibles of a rather different kind. We (Victor, his friend and her daughter) found ourselves outside looking for tracks left by those who'd visited us the night before (see "Grays" on page 33). Victor had brought the camcorder, and I had my ever-present camera with me. He was looking through the viewfinder while he was scanning the area. Just as he walked toward a nearby fence, he exclaimed, "Mom! What are those pigs doing here? See them?" I looked in the direction in which he pointed but couldn't see anything out of the ordinary. "Right there!" he exclaimed, and he pointed to a spot directly in front of us. There was nothing but the ground, the fence and a dry wash with tall brush beyond.

In frustration, Victor looked up from the viewfinder and,

incredulously, found that he couldn't see the pigs anymore. He returned to the viewfinder and found he could see them again. "I tell you, they're there!" He filmed a very short piece and asked us to follow him into the house. Once inside, he put the tape in the VCR, and sure enough, there were pigs!

These were not the wild javelina indigenous to that area, but domestic pigs. There were no domestic pigs within fifteen miles of the ranch, yet there on the tape, plain as day, was a sow's head and a small piglet. Were these perhaps entities who had shape-shifted, or was this a dimensional bleed-through? I still don't know, but the pigs sure made for many hours of contemplation and conversation.

Physiology

To evolve into mastery, one must understand the workings of one's vehicle [body] in relation to All That Is. One's body is grand indeed, as it takes one about one's business of life on Earth. As you know by this time, you, as essence, are living within the outer shell, which is an outer reflection of you. You, the true you, are Spirit.

The human body is a complex mechanism, but we will bring about a simple understanding of it. All life is a composite of electromagnetism. Everything, seen and unseen, is a mass of molecular particles ever moving, never stopping. This movement of life is charged and propelled by a form of electromagnetic energy. Even the planet on which you reside is embedded with this energy.

There are varying degrees of this electrical energy, and these degrees determine how dense or etheric life is there. All energy resonates to like energy. You, our one, have photographed beings who, not seen by the physical eye, could be picked up by the eye and lens of your camera. You could "feel" the energy of these beings, and yet you could not physically see them. The camera, with its quick eye and ability to instantaneously capture ▶

an image, could record them for you. Most upon your plane cannot see these etheric beings for the reason that their own energy is the same as that in your dimension. Their physical eyes can see no further.

Now, do you recall when you discovered that at times you could faintly see these entities with your eyes? Why is that? That is because as you evolve spiritually, your energy—your electromagnetic energy—is escalated, bringing you to a slightly elevated space to which you had not been before. For a time you are not totally resonant to your dimension. As your energy heightens, your ability to see these beings is clarified. You are more closely resonating to their vibrational pattern.

In the aspect of quantum physics, as it is known there, it is understood that there are multiple dimensions that share the same space-time continuum. That is to say that these dimensions are able to be in the same space without awareness of the others. These varying dimensions are vibrating at different frequencies. Those in your dimension upon Earth are all vibrating at a certain decibel. Magnetically, this binds all of that vibrational level together. Always remember, like attracts like.

As one grows within and opens one's heart, a change takes form in the aspect of one's vibrational level. The vibrations escalate. Do you recall hearing of masters upon your plane who have the ability to disappear before one's eyes? No mystery here . . . they are merely vibrating at will at a higher level, which allows them to slip into another dimension that is compatible with their current magnetic energy. Very simple, is it not? What of those who have the ability to bilocate? You might see this being in front of you, and yet this one is reported as being seen elsewhere at the same time. These ones have the capability to split off their energy at will and be two places at the same time.

What of the beings you photographed? No difference

here! They merely *lowered* their vibrational level to arrive in your dimension. It is far easier to heighten one's vibration than to lower it. This is why those who lower their energies do not remain in your dimension for long.

There is also another instance of experiencing the beings who you could not see and yet "felt." This was due not to a changing of their vibrational level but of yours. You were able to momentarily slip into their dimension.

When does mastery become a part of this? Only when one truly understands the simplicity of these actions and is able to alter one's frequencies at will. In your case, one, it was an instantaneous happening, which you did not consciously bring about.

With this knowledge comes an enormous responsibility. This is why vibrational alterations should come about *only* through spiritual growth. One must be shed of many things. We will list a few. There can be no ego, no selfish ulterior motives, no voyeurism. This is not a license to look in upon others with anything but a pure heart. That which one must have is again a pure heart, which encompasses unselfishness with only the will of the Father in mind. For one to manipulate one's vibrational pattern for any reason other than this is dealt with harshly.

At this point, may we state that the altering of vibrational frequencies is but a mere fraction of a master's ability. In truth, it is very low on the list of importance. The greatest masters can do is shed their light to all within the realm around them. This light—and only this light—is of major importance. We mainly bring about this subject of vibrational frequencies to explain why some experience unseen beings around them and how this is possible.

The subject of electromagnetic vibrational properties is applicable to all life, both seen and unseen.

CHAPTER THREE

MORE VISITORS

Oftentimes my messengers helped me come to terms with what I experienced. Even if they did not offer detailed explanations for the incidents that happened on Bradshaw Ranch, they usually provided much help and information. However, when I looked for guidance in my encounters with ETs, all I received was the terse message titled "Visitors," printed at the end of this chapter. This was not enough. ETs were frequent visitors to both my son Victor and me, and Victor was even abducted (his experience is described in *Merging Dimensions*). Why would my messengers not share more information about them?

In time I understood that this was for me to learn on my own, through my experiences. To further my growth, I needed to come to my own conclusions from within rather than be given knowledge forthright. My messengers preferred to place road signs upon my path. The turns I took were my choice and my choice alone.

Some people have traumatic experiences with extraterrestrial visitors, and I want to be the first to say that these experiences are valid. However, there is far more to be understood about this issue that, for some, these visits by extraterrestrials have negative connotations, whereas others talk only about experiencing love and peace.

Photographer: © Victor Johnson.

◀ VICTOR WAS PHOTOGRAPHING HIS FRIEND. NOTICE THE ENERGY ABOVE HIS HEAD, SURROUNDING AN ORB OF LIGHT.

◀ THE ENERGY, ALSO SHOWN IN THE ▼ PHOTO BELOW, APPEARS IN A DUSTY MAUVE COLOR. (REFER TO COLOR PLATES).

VICTOR'S FRIEND.

Photographer: © Linda Ball.

FIRELIKE LIGHT ENERGY.

We are told that we are cocreators. In other words, we can and do create with our thoughts. The door is open for us to choose what we create with our inner thoughts, beliefs and identity. Until we truly understand the power we have through our spiritual connection, we are going to create negative experiences.

Consciously, some victims of abductions are not aware of their cocreator abilities, and they are truly traumatized but do not know why. They are actually experiencing pain, both emotionally and physically. The missing key is the ability to pull forth from their superconsciousness the equipment they have to change their experience: the willingness to see themselves for who they truly are and not who they assume themselves to be.

I speak of this as one with firsthand experience. I too went through traumatic experiences when I was confronted by some of these beings. In time, however, I grew to understand the basis of my experiences, and I chose to bring forth my true self. When I did this, the darkness completely vanished. This sounds simple, but it takes a great desire on one's part to grow weary of the pain. We do not have to be victims. Please do not see this statement as placing myself above others. I know, in truth, that we are all equal. With the realization of this equality as truth comes the knowledge that one's perspective can be altered to change terrifying experiences into positive ones.

You are much greater than you realize and much more powerful than you imagine. Take the time to introduce yourself to *you*, the true you, and see where your true identity stems from. As an enlightened being, there is no power that can overpower you.

Beautiful Beings

It would have been easy to get caught up in the more negative aspects of the phenomena if it had not been for our encounters with all the peaceful beings who visited the ranch. In fact, the "good" experiences far outweighed the not-so-good. Wherever these peaceful beings appeared, a cloak of serenity seemed to cover the entire area. It was almost as if time stood still, and I found myself absorbing the love that permeated all space around them.

As he often did, my son, Victor, slept on the sofa in the living room rather than in the adobe house where he lived. Something woke him up, and he saw a tall, ethereal form coming from the hallway that led to the master bedroom where I was sleeping. To this day, my son maintains that this being emanated the greatest love he has ever experienced in his lifetime, a love completely different from what we as humans normally express to one another.

The approximately seven-foot-tall form was somewhat luminous and wore a long, blue robe. His eyes were a bit sunken in, and his sharp facial features were framed by short, black hair and sideburns. His hair was cropped close to his head, shorter on the forehead than at the sides. Victor's detailed description of the being reminded me of the being we had called the Blue Man, and I am certain both beings were of the same race; maybe they were even the same being.

While he lay there wide awake in amazement, the beautiful being expressed to him telepathically that he should not be afraid, for he was in no danger. Although he could not remember the exact words, my son recalled that the being told him that he knew us and visited often. Victor was left with the impression that this entity loved us very much, and he also received the message that he would be taught what he needed to know by this being: "We will teach you." The glowing entity then crossed the living room and floated through a wall as my son watched.

As soon as the being left the living room, Victor jumped up and threw back the drapes, which covered the window above the sofa. Outside, in addition to the tall being, he saw a smaller one next to my truck, which was parked near the house. The tall being disappeared while the smaller being, who was only about four feet tall, turned to look at Victor and telepathically requested that he follow. Victor stayed where he was, at the living room window, and watched the being as it lifted one knee, wrapped its arms around the uplifted knee, ducked its head and transformed into a ball of

Photographer: © Linda Ball.

THE BEING WHO INVITED VICTOR TO FOLLOW TRANSFORMED ITSELF AND THEN RESEMBLED THE ORBS OF LIGHT WE SO OFTEN ENCOUNTERED.

light, which then disappeared. Perhaps these were some of the light orbs we saw so often. It certainly would explain the sense of peace we experienced whenever they were near.

One morning I awoke early, at 3:50 A.M. as a look at the clock told me. I don't know what woke me, and although it was still dark, I couldn't go back to sleep. Instead I had the strong feeling that I should get up and look out the window of the bedroom door that led directly outside. As I peeked outside, I saw a white mass near the horses' water troughs, which were located just left of our water tank. I blinked and looked again. It was still there, a mass of white light approximately two feet taller than the split-rail fence posts, which made it about my height (I am five feet three inches tall). The form moved fluidly, appearing first as an indistinct mass, then taking on form. It turned slowly and what resembled arms extended out on either side. Bending over at the waist, the form seemed to be doing something on the ground. It rose, then repeated the process a number of times as I looked on.

Photographer: © Linda Ball.

LIGHT ENERGY APPEARING ABOVE ONE OF OUR DOGS, PATCHES. NOTE THE MYSTERIOUS SHADOW TO THE RIGHT OF PATCHES.

For more than an hour I watched as the mass changed form, from a ghostly mass to an ill-defined body to a big ball of light, then back to a body, then back to a mass. It appeared rather wispy, yet at times became more dense. As I watched, three times a small light appeared right in the middle of its form, then disappeared. The light fluctuated from red to green to white. More balls and pinpoints of light appeared and remained close to the form. At one point, a ball of light appeared directly in front of the window through which I watched, and I got the distinct impression that it, in turn, was

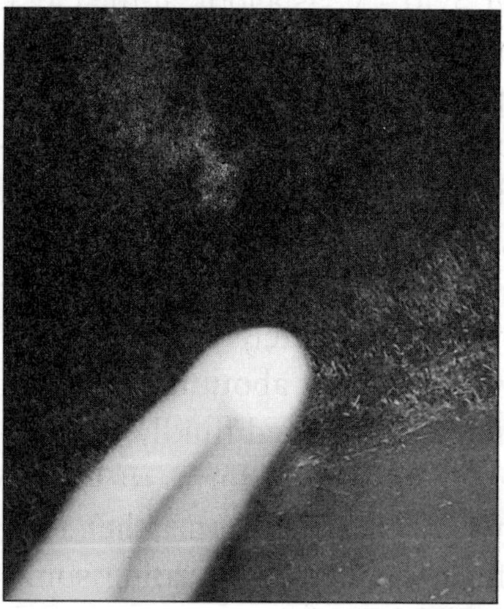

Photographer: © Linda Ball.

THESE FAST-MOVING ORBS WITH "CONTRAILS" ON TWO SIDES WERE NOT AN UNCOMMON OCCURRENCE.

watching *me*. The ball disappeared quickly, and a cometlike streak of light shot straight through the air not far from the white form, perhaps four feet above the ground.

Occasionally, the white form flickered like a fluorescent bulb and became less dense. It was then that I could see tubular forms within the outer shape. One time, as it flickered thus, I made out three tubular forms with a ball of light above them. When it stopped flickering, the form once again obtained an almost human, yet cloudlike shape. Above its head I observed an electrical arc such as the one you see when photographing lightning. Shortly after that, the arc disappeared and a tubular light above the form's head took its place. It was magnificent.

Just about then I spotted a craft approaching from the north. It moved extremely slowly, unlike any regular aircraft, finding its way to the hill on the west side of the ranch, then gradually lowering itself below the skyline as if preparing to land.

I've watched these craft perform such maneuvers before, but something was different this time: Just before the craft dipped below the horizon, it emitted an incredible halo of light all around it. The halo resembled pictures of sunbursts, and I distinctly remember seeing silvery spikes of light. All of this happened very quickly, and before I knew it, the light seemed to draw itself back into the craft.

I considered stepping outside with my camera, but I knew the white form would sense my presence even if I didn't make any noise. From my vantage point at the window a tree was somewhat in the way, prohibiting the use of a camera. To watch, I had to peer out the window panes at a weird angle, which made my neck a bit stiff. I resigned to record what I saw mentally rather than risk scaring the form off.

I must emphasize that I was wide awake during these events; this was not a dream. At one point, I went to the living room where Victor was sleeping and tried to wake him up. What I was witnessing was so incredible, and I wanted to share it with him. I tried rousing him once, twice, three times, but the only thing I achieved was that he moved slightly, mumbled and returned to his deep sleep. This was curious, since it was not like Victor to sleep so deeply. I gave up my attempts to wake him and returned to my vantage point by the window of the door to continue watching the phenomena.

What was this white form? Was it a hologram? A life form? I still do not know. Whatever it was, however, it was fascinating to witness.

Grays

One experience will stand out in my memory forever. Even now, as I reflect back on it, it appears almost surreal.

One summer evening, Victor was entertaining a lady friend and her then seven-year-old daughter. The three stayed in the small, usually unoccupied house at the north end of the ranch. At approximately a quarter to three in the morning my son was still awake and happened to be looking out a north-facing window when he spotted a round, metallic, saucer-shaped UFO landing nearby. He whispered to his friend to get her attention, and the two of them stared out the window, watching intently as the lights edged downward. They weren't quite prepared for what they saw next.

Strolling right past the window were four aliens! Disbelievingly, Victor and his friend stared at the somewhat short-statured extraterrestrials, who wore tight-fitting, one-piece uniforms in a light tan color. Once the aliens were out of sight and the witnesses had recomposed themselves, they woke the young child. The three of them jumped into Victor's car and sped to the house where I was sleeping. I remember so vividly how my son vigorously shook my arm to wake me up. I can still hear the trepidation in his voice as he said, "Mom, wake up! They're here!" Startled, yet still half asleep, I raised up and asked, "Who's here?" "The aliens, Mom!"

Needless to say, I jumped out of bed like a streak of lightning and hurried into the living room where I found the young woman and her daughter sitting on the sofa in a state of shock. Victor gave me a breathless rundown of what had happened, then I too sat on the sofa, dumbfounded. Realizing it was going to be a long night, I pulled myself together and went to the kitchen to put on some coffee.

When I returned to the living room, Victor's friend was pointing to the front door, sputtering, "There . . . there's one now!" I looked out the windows of the front door, and sure enough, an alien was walking past the door across the small porch. The alien looked like one of the Grays, typically called the Zeta Reticuli, only this one appeared to be a bit more ashen-colored, almost white. I'm not certain what came over me, but I raced past the others and reached for the door (most likely the time had come to prevail over my fear). Concerned about my safety, my son grabbed me by the arm and yelled, "What are you doing? You can't go out there!" Pulling away from his grip, I confidently answered, "They can't hurt me," and opened the door and went out into the yard.

Our visitors seemed to disappear the moment I joined them outside. But I could still feel their intense presence, and once my eyes had adjusted to the dark, I could also see a faint outline of their shapes. At this point, I was incensed more than anything. How dare they intrude upon our space and then have the audacity to transform to a state in which they could see me but I could barely see them! I asked that they identify themselves. There was no audible or telepathic response. To give them another option, I asked that they at least tap something three times if they were of the light. Again, there was no response, but I could still make out the vague outlines of their forms. Since they were not willing to communicate, I ordered them to leave. They stepped back a great distance but remained in the area. Once more I commanded their departure. Then they were gone.

Probably they returned to their craft, which they had left at the north end of the ranch, and took off. Things quieted down after that, but needless to say, we did not attempt to go back to sleep.

I am not an expert on aliens, and I don't profess to know their agenda. There is a lot of conjecture about the intentions of these Grays. Many say they are of the dark or have a sinister plan for us. This may be so, or it may not. I can only draw from my own experience with them, and they did not leave me with a particularly good feeling. However, this does not imply that I felt in any kind of danger. At no time during this experience was there any indication from our visitors that they intended to harm either myself or my family.

I have learned that I must gauge each experience and each encounter by the feelings I have at the time they happen. It is so easy to become overzealous with preconceived notions and allow these to direct rather than be led by one's own inner guidance. How sad if one should meet an angel or being of spiritual light and command it to leave only because it is invisible or nearly invisible. Discernment is key.

The Tan Guy

As was often our habit, Tom and I were walking within the vicinity of the area we had come to believe was a doorway or portal. There were times when we could distinctly feel activity around us, as if a light electrical current was flowing through the air. That evening was one of those times, and we tuned in to any activity both in the sky and around us.

We knew with certainty that something was going on, and yet we could not visualize anything. Being incurably curious, we persevered, convinced that some sort of occurrence would evolve. And then it happened.

Tom pointed to an area just a few feet from us and said, "Linda! Right there! Do you see him?" I quickly looked to where he was pointing, and I saw him. There, right in front of us, was a being, perhaps four to four-and-a-half feet tall, running very quickly away from us. He was not in full density, yet we could see him clearly. He was wearing what appeared to be a one-piece, tightly fitting garment, which was light tan in color. We could see only the back of him, but from that perspective his form appeared to be very human. He was running across an open field, and then within seconds we watched him slip through what I can only describe as an invisible wall. Logically we knew there was nothing in that field; yet as our eyes were fixed upon him he disappeared, one section of his body at a time, soon to be totally gone from our view.

Tom and I looked at each other in wonderment, and then we slowly walked to the area where the alien had disappeared. There was nothing—at least nothing we could see or sense. Both of us had cameras with us, but the encounter had happened so quickly that there was no time to catch our sprinting visitor on film.

Visitors

Yes, one, shall we talk of visitors? It has come to your attention that there are beings arriving in your dimension who do not permanently reside there. These are the ones many of your plane call aliens. The term "alien" has a broad spectrum and in reality encompasses any being who is not of a territorial area. Thusly, this could also encompass what many of your realm call angels or highly evolved beings. For this lesson, shall we focus upon those who are mainly perceived as arriving in ships or "UFOs," to use a common term?

Do humans have the audacity to perceive that their species is exclusive to the universe? This thought process brings about an aura of superiority, which is not truth.

Indeed, there are additional species who live and function in other realms or dimensions . . . perhaps on other planets. ▶

Are they negative or evil? Or perchance, are they beings who have chosen to arrive in the form of "savior," as many upon your plane perceive? Reports of abductions are given, with accusations that these visitors exercise abuse or dominion upon humans. Other reports are given, with statements that the human experiences only love and enlightenment. Which theorist is right? Neither and both. Do recall that one creates one's life experiences with one's perspectives. Tell me, if a ship landed before you today, what would your experience encompass? Recall that you are the screenwriter of this movie.

Are they negative or evil? Or perchance, are there beings who have chosen to arrive in the form of "[illegible]" [illegible] our planet [illegible]? Reports of abductions [illegible] [illegible] [illegible] [illegible] [illegible] [illegible] [illegible] [illegible] [illegible] [illegible] [illegible] [illegible] [illegible] [illegible]

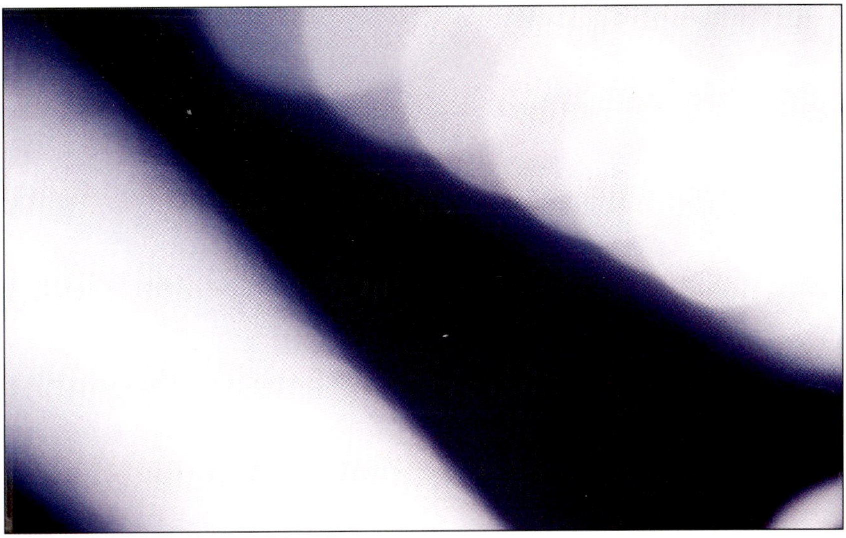

Photographer: © Linda Ball.

1 Close-up of fast-moving orbs.

The colors of the light orbs ranged from white, pink, a pale red and orange to blue and various shades in between. They emitted a sense of peace and tranquillity whenever they were in close proximity.

Photographer: © Linda Ball.

2 Orbs of light with truck; Tom Dongo in the front and Jim Sweel in the background.

Photographer: © Linda Ball.

3 MULTI-COLORED ORBS OF LIGHT.

Photographer: © Linda Ball.

4 ORBS OVER GROUND.

Photographer: © Linda Ball.

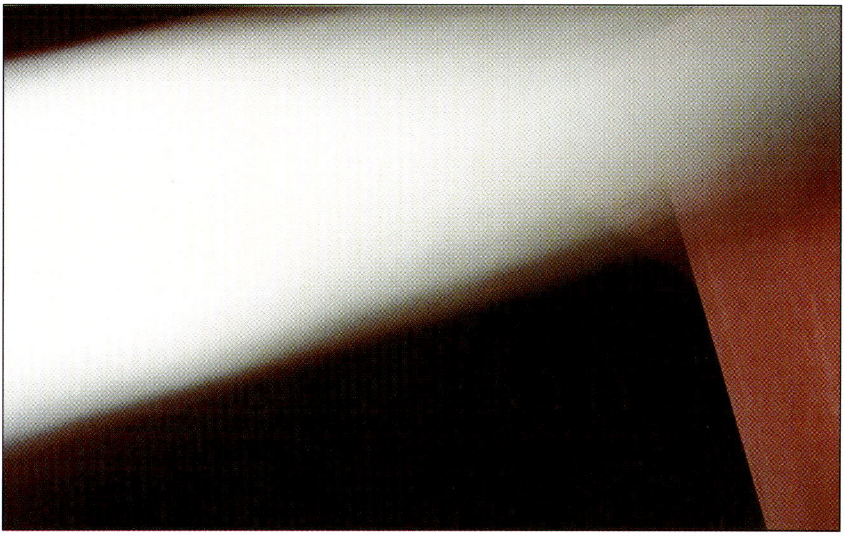

5 FAST-MOVING LIGHT ENERGY ZIPPING BY THE HOUSE.

Photographer: © Linda Ball.

6 ENERGY ZIPPING BY AT AN INCREDIBLE SPEED.

Photographer: © Linda Ball.

7 STREAM OF LIGHT IN FRONT OF TREE.

THESE STREAMS OR STREAKS OF LIGHT APPEARED OFTEN, AND WITH THEM WE SENSED A MORE INTENSE ENERGY AS THEY ZIPPED PAST AT AN INCREDIBLE SPEED.

Photographer: © Linda Ball.

8 STREAM OF LIGHT IN FRONT OF THE OLD ADOBE HOMESTEAD.

Photographer: © Linda Ball.

9 MULTITUDES OF ORBS BY THE RANCH HOUSE.

AT TIMES THE LIGHT ORBS APPEARED IN LARGE NUMBERS. I TOOK THESE PHOTOS ON A DRY, CLEAR NIGHT.

Photographer: © Linda Ball.

10 MULTITUDES OF ORBS OVER TREE AND FIELD.

Photographer: © Linda Ball.

11 ORB OF LIGHT HOVERING BY A FENCE.

Photographer: © Linda Ball.

12 TOM HAD ASKED ME TO PHOTOGRAPH HIM AS HE MEDITATED, ENVISIONING AN ORB OF LIGHT. THE ORB DID APPEAR.

Photographer: © Linda Ball.

13 FAST-MOVING ENERGY SKIMMING ABOVE THE GROUND.

Photographer: © Linda Ball.

14 FAST-MOVING ENERGY BETWEEN THE HOUSE AND TREE.

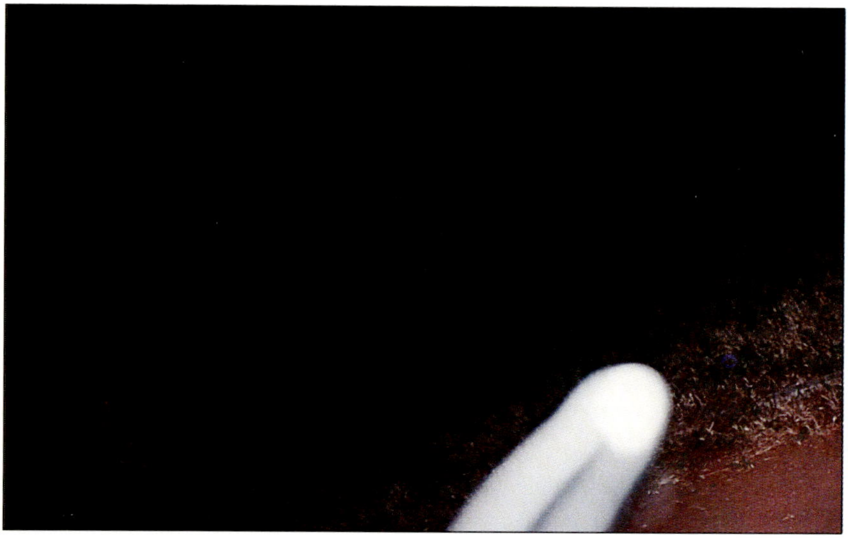

Photographer: © Linda Ball.

15 THESE FAST-MOVING ORBS WITH "CONTRAILS" ON TWO SIDES WERE NOT AN UNCOMMON OCCURRENCE.

Photographer: © Linda Ball.

16 FAST ORB MOVING UPWARDS, PAST VICTOR'S TRUCK.

17 ENERGY STREAMING OUT OF WHITE FORM.

18 CIRCULAR ENERGY WITH WHITE ORB BENEATH IT.

Photographer: © Linda Ball.

19 ENERGY ZIPPING BY AT AN INCREDIBLE SPEED.

Photographer: © Linda Ball.

20 MORE ENERGY ZIPPING BY AT AN INCREDIBLE SPEED.

Photographer: © Linda Ball.

21 FAST-MOVING LIGHT ENERGY ZIPPING EITHER AWAY FROM OR TOWARD THE HOUSE.

Photographer: © Linda Ball.

22 ORBS OVER FENCE.

Photographer: © Linda Ball.

23 HOVERING ORB, BY THE RANCH HOUSE.

Photographer: © Linda Ball.

24 LIGHT ANOMALIES IN VARIOUS COLORS, WITH BROKEN OR SCALLOPED PERIMETERS.

Photographer: © Linda Ball.

25 WAFTING ORB NEAR THE PROPANE TANK.

Photographer: © Linda Ball.

26 ORB OVER GROUND.

Photographer: © Tom Dongo.

27 TOM'S PHOTO OF THE FIRST HUMANOID BEING CAUGHT ONLY THE TOP OF THE BEING'S HEAD FROM THE FRONT, WITH HAIR FALLING SIDEWAYS OVER THE FOREHEAD.

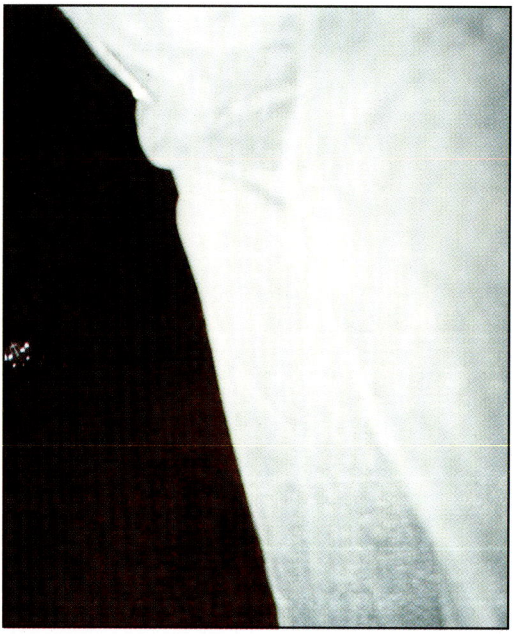

Photographer: © Tom Dongo.

28 NOTE THE SMALL OBJECT HOVERING BY THE BEING'S LEGS.

THE SECOND PHOTO TOM TOOK OF THIS FIRST HUMANOID BEING SHOWS A DEFINITE BODY FROM THE STOMACH DOWN, PHOTOGRAPHED FROM THE SIDE.

THE SMALL OBJECT HOVERING BY THE BEING'S LEGS APPEARED AGAIN, NEXT TO ANOTHER, TOTALLY DIFFERENT BEING WE DUBBED THE "BLUE MAN" (PHOTO 30).

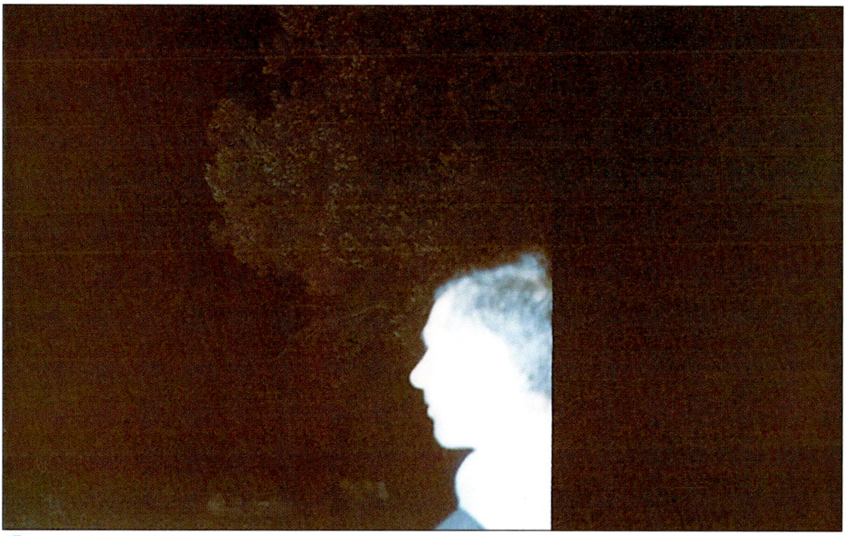

Photographer: © Linda Ball.

29 THE BLUE MAN'S UPPER TORSO AND HEAD. NOTE THE PALE BLUE TINGE TO THE FACE AND THE EAR.

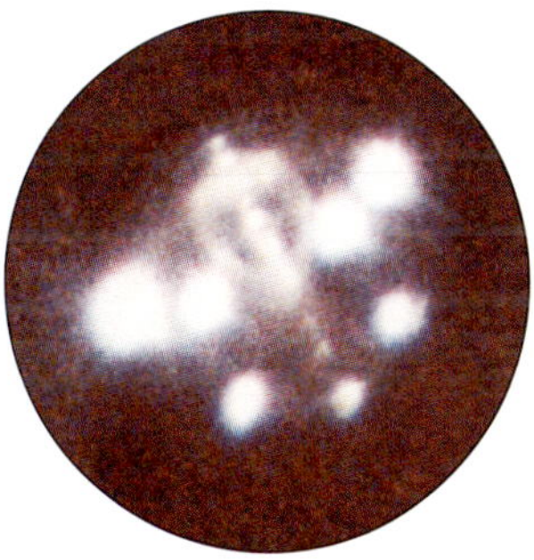

▲ NOTE THE OBJECT HOVERING BY THE BEING'S LEG. IT IS THE SAME OBJECT WE SAW BY THE FIRST HUMANLIKE BEING (PHOTO 28)

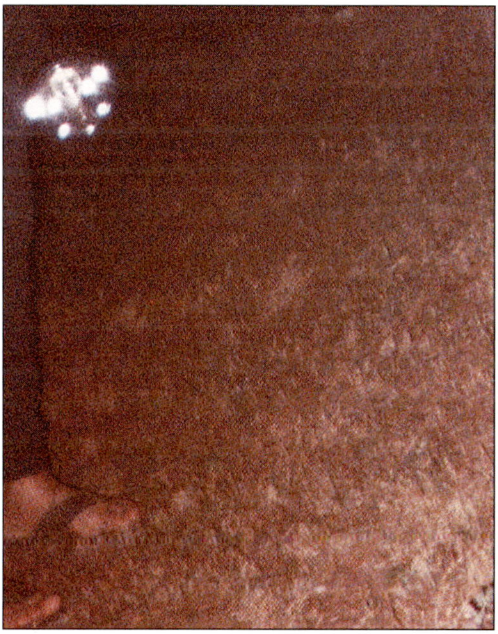

Photographer: © Tom Dongo.

30 THE BLUE MAN'S LEG AND FEET.

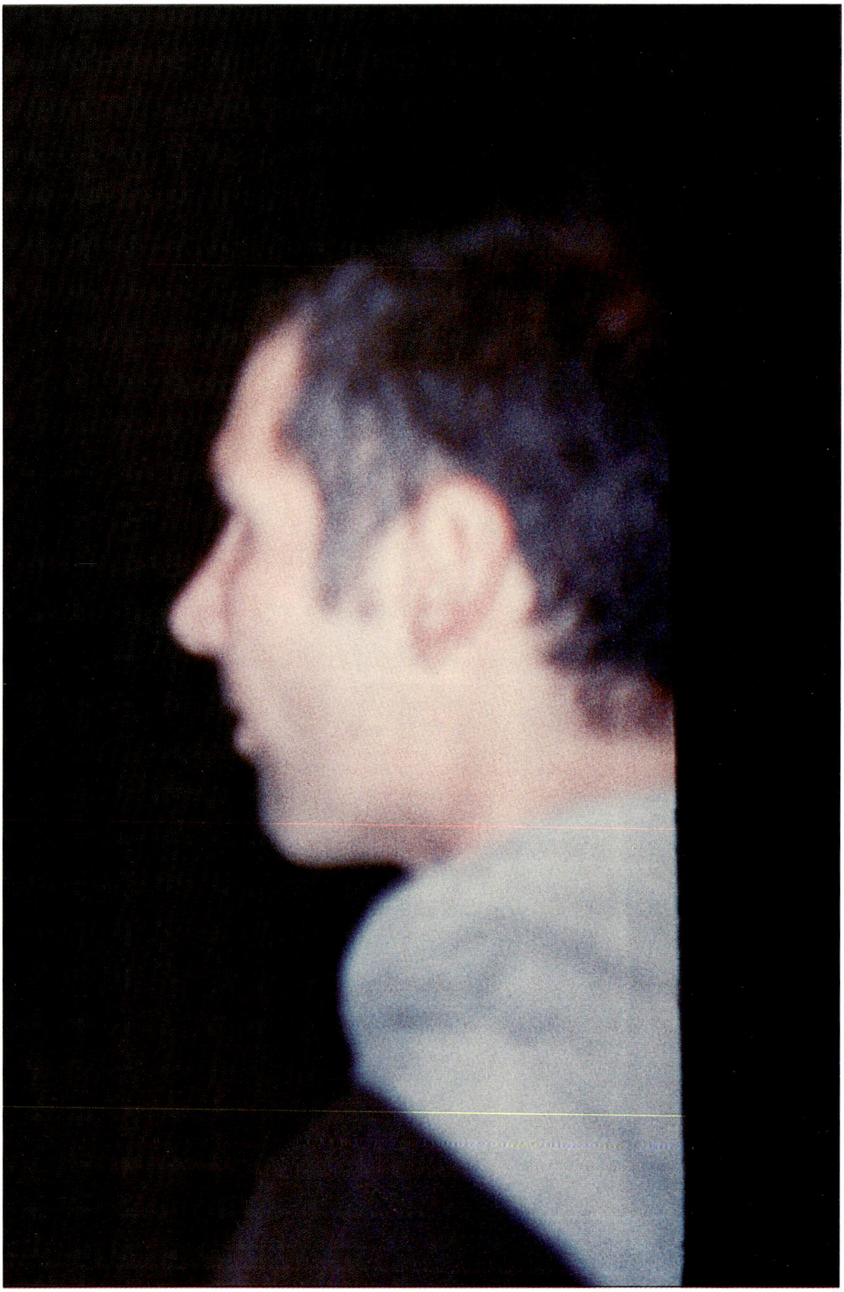

Photographer: © Linda 3all.

31 ENLARGEMENT OF THE BLUE MAN. THE BEING'S EAR OPENING APPEARS TO BE AT THE TOP RATHER THAN THE BOTTOM, AND THERE IS A RIPPLED RIDGE OF CARTILAGE ALONG THE OUTSIDE EDGE AND ON THE BOTTOM.

32 The Blue Man's physical body has disappeared, and in its stead is this quickly moving streak of light. Note the density of form within it.

Photographer: © Linda Ball.

Photographer: © Linda Ball.

33 THE BEING WHO LEFT THE PRINTS APPEARED TO HAVE ONE VERY POINTED APPENDAGE WITH A SHORT, WIDE DIGIT NEXT TO IT.

Photographer: © Linda Ball.

34 THE LEFT SIDE OF THE CAMERA.

Photographer: © Unknown.

35 THIS SHOT SHOWS THE CEILING LIGHT IN THE KITCHEN. IT APPEARS TO BE TURNED ON WITH NO ILLUMINATION SURROUNDING IT.

THESE SHOTS WERE TAKEN INSIDE THE HOUSE, MOSTLY AT NIGHTTIME. HOW STRANGE . . . I KNEW I HAD NOT TAKEN ANY INTERIOR SHOTS.

Photographer: © Unknown.

36 THE KITCHEN LIGHTS ARE "ON" WITH ONLY A DIM, RUSSET-COLORED HUE VISIBLE IN THE ROOM.

Photographer: © Unknown.

37 KITCHEN AND TREE OUTSIDE, EVERYTHING DISTORTED.

Photographer: © Linda Ball.

38 UNKNOWN ENERGY EMITTING FROM WHITE FORM.

Photographer: © Linda Ball.

39 THE BEING WHO INVITED VICTOR TO FOLLOW TRANSFORMED ITSELF AND THEN RESEMBLED THE ORBS OF LIGHT WE SO OFTEN ENCOUNTERED.

Photographer: © Linda Ball.

40 LIGHT ENERGY APPEARING ABOVE ONE OF OUR DOGS, PATCHES. NOTE THE MYSTERIOUS SHADOW TO THE RIGHT OF PATCHES.

Photographer: © Victor Johnson.

41 VICTOR'S FRIEND.

◀ VICTOR WAS PHOTOGRAPHING HIS FRIEND. NOTICE THE ENERGY ABOVE HIS HEAD, SURROUNDING AN ORB OF LIGHT.

▼ THE PHOTO BELOW SHOWS THE SAME DUSTY MAUVE COLOR THAT APPEARED ABOVE VICTOR'S FRIEND

Photographer: © Linda Ball.

42 FIRELIKE LIGHT ENERGY.

Photographer: © Linda Ball.

43 ORANGE STREAKS BEAMING FROM THE SKY DOWN ONTO VICTOR'S TRUCK.

Photographer: © Linda Ball.

44 BEAUTIFUL HUE OF LIGHT WAFTING IN FRONT OF ME.

Photographer: © Linda Ball.

45 THIS IS WHAT IS COMMONLY CALLED A WINDOW.

Photographer: © Linda Ball.

46 ANOTHER WINDOW WITH AN ORB TO THE LEFT OF IT.

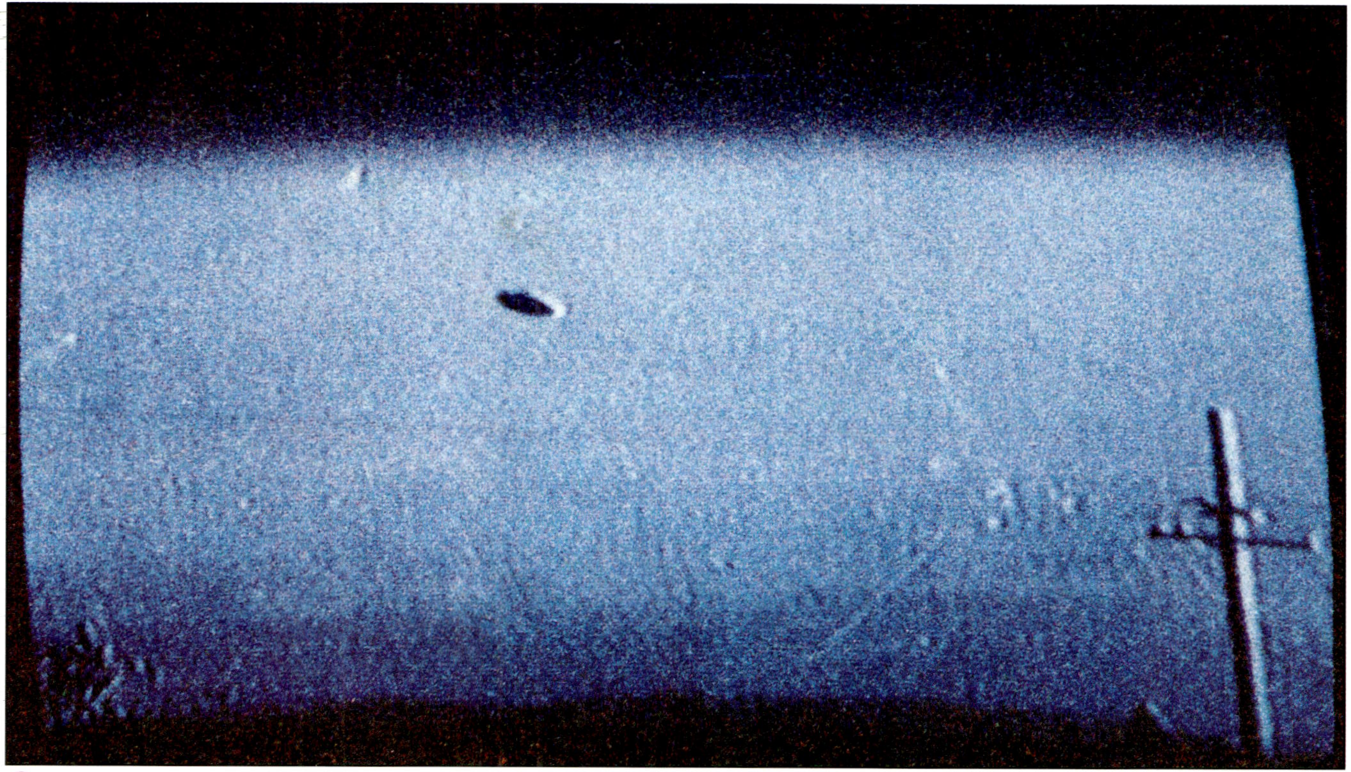

Photographer: © Linda Ball.

47 Enlargement of the "window" I captured on film when the large box of light appeared just a few feet above me. Notice the several components: a humanoid figure in the lower left corner, a saucer-shaped craft in the center and what could be a telephone pole or the mast of a sailboat in the lower right corner.

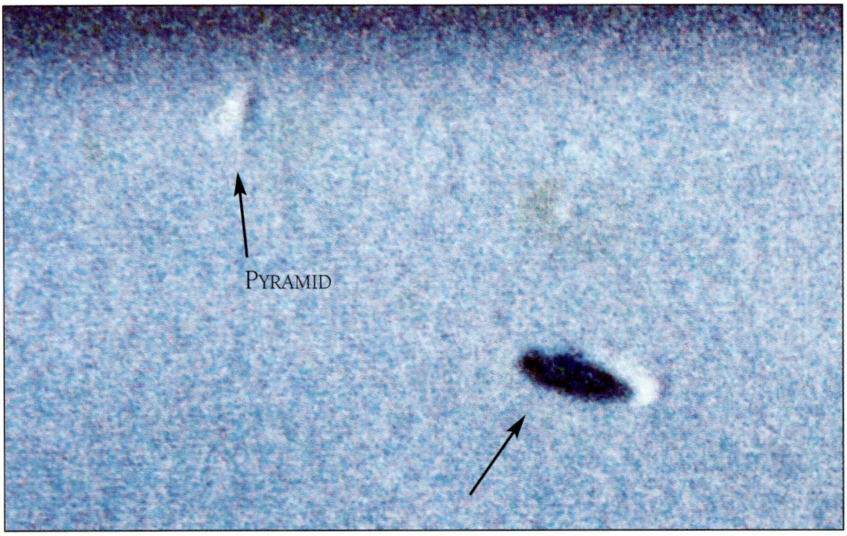

Photographer: © Linda Ball.

47a CLOSE-UP OF PYRAMID AND SAUCER-SHAPED CRAFT.

Photographer: © Linda Ball.

47b CLOSE-UP OF HUMANOID.

◀ THE LOWER LEFT CORNER OF THE PHOTO SHOWS A HUMANOID, WHO SEEMS TO HAVE SOMETHING CRADLED IN THE LEFT ARM WHILE REACHING FOR SOMETHING WITH THE RIGHT HAND. THE HUMANOID IS LOOKING TO THE LEFT.

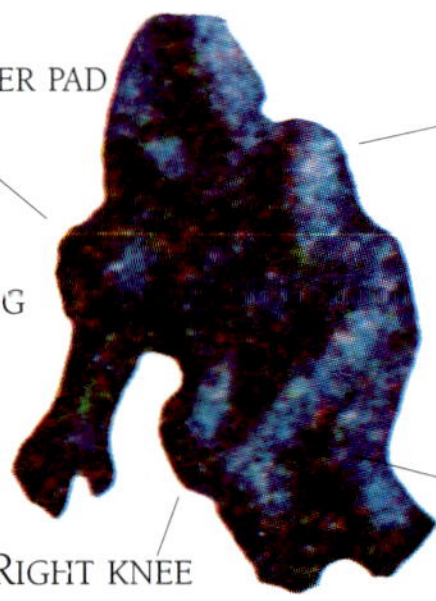

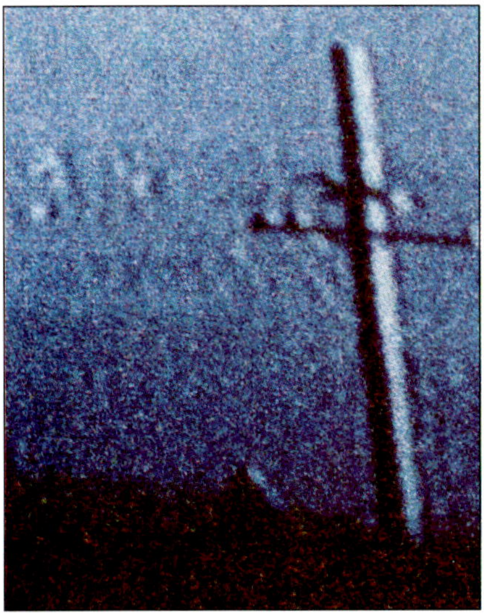

Photographer: © Linda Ball.

47c CLOSE-UP OF OBJECT SIMILAR TO A TELEPHONE POLE OR SHIP'S MAST.

◀ THERE WERE NO TELEPHONE POLES ON THE RANCH; THE NEAREST ONE WAS ONE MILE AWAY.

WHAT I HAD PHOTOGRAPHED THAT NIGHT WAS WHAT IS COMMONLY TERMED A "WINDOW." THESE ARE AREAS WHERE THE VEIL BETWEEN DIMENSIONS IS VERY THIN, THEREBY ALLOWING A RESIDENT OF ONE DIMENSION EASIER ACCESS TO FREQUENCIES IN OTHER DIMENSIONS. IN FACT, MOST OF MY ENCOUNTERS WITH BEINGS FROM OTHER WORLDS TOOK PLACE EITHER DIRECTLY BENEATH THAT OPENING OR VERY CLOSE TO IT.

▼ SHAPES TO THE LEFT OF THE POLE/MAST RESEMBLE A FLYING BAT AND THE NUMBER 39, FOLLOWED BY A DOT. THESE SHAPES ARE HIGHLIGHTED BELOW.

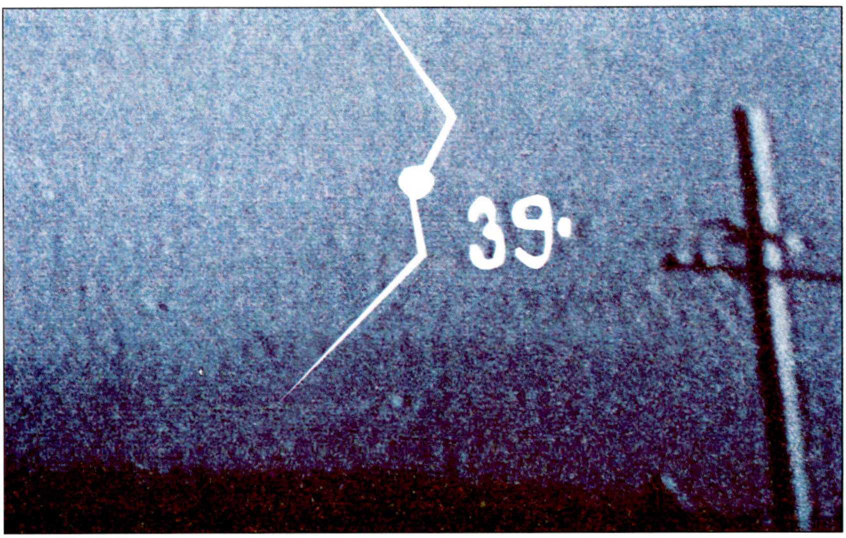

Photographer: © Linda Ball.

47d POSSIBLE POLE OR MAST. NOTE THE SHAPES DIRECTLY TO THE LEFT OF IT.

Photographer: © Linda Ball.

48 INTENSE ENERGY WITH FAINT, WHITE WINDOW IN ITS CENTER. NOTE THE BLUE ORB TO THE LEFT.

Photographer: © Linda Ba l.

49 STREAM OF ENERGY IN FRONT OF THE ADOBE HOUSE. NOTE THE ORB IN THE ENERGY'S BOTTOM CENTER.

50 THIS FLAME WHIZZED PAST US, JUST A FEW FEET AWAY.

Photographer: © Tom Dongo.

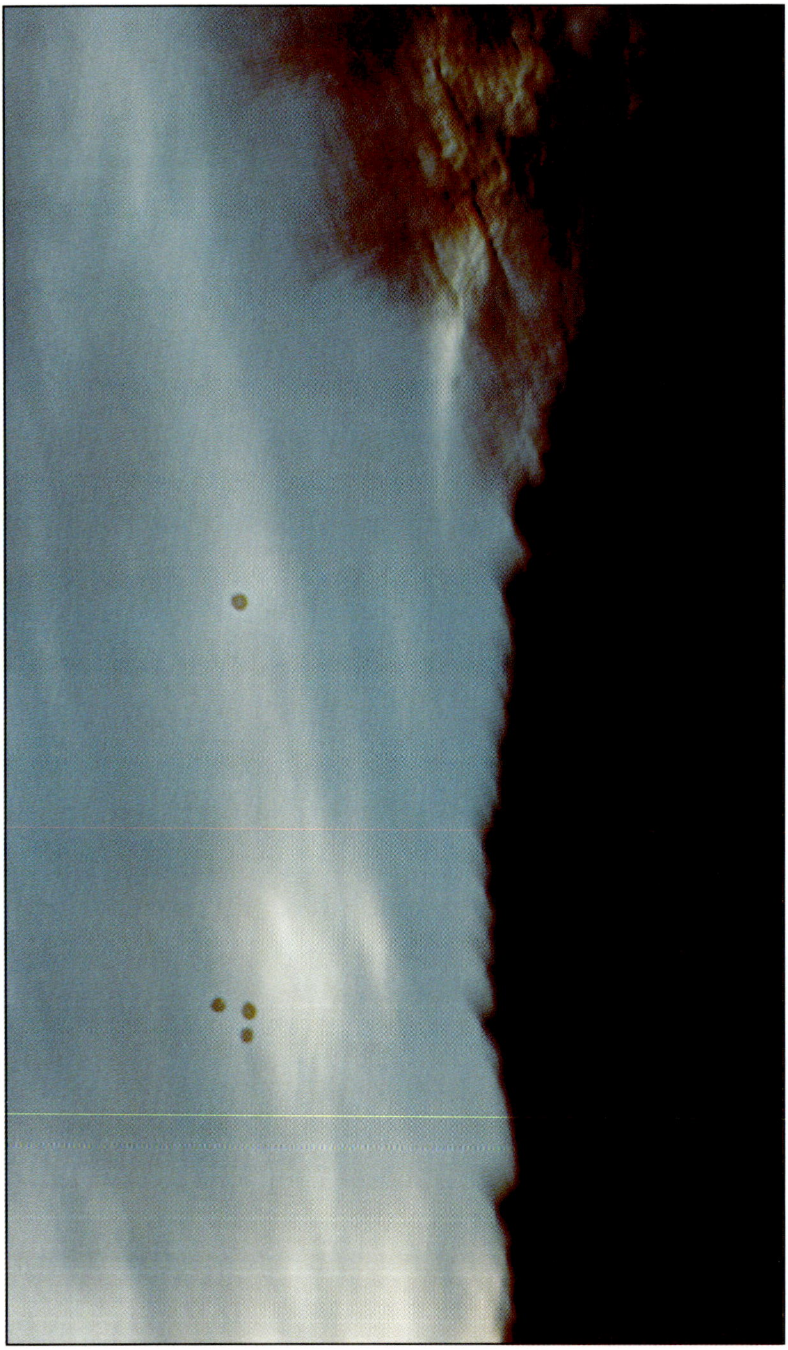

51 GOLDEN BALLS OF LIGHT THAT APPEARED WHILE I WAS ENACTING A PHOTO SESSION FOR *PARANORMAL BORDERLINE.*

Photographer: © Linda Ball.

Photographer: © Linda Ball.

52 I STRONGLY SUSPECTED THAT THE HISSING INTRUDER AND OTHERS LIKE IT LEFT THESE PRINTS, WHICH WERE APPROXIMATELY FOURTEEN INCHES LONG. THEY AVERAGED ABOUT EIGHT INCHES IN WIDTH AT THE TOES AND NARROWED TO A POINT AT THE HEEL.

Photographer: © Linda Ball.

53 LARGE PRINT FOUND ALONGSIDE HASSAYAMPA RIVER WHILE EXPLORING WITH FRIENDS. NOTE THE SIMILARITY TO THE PRINT I FOUND ON BRADSHAW RANCH (TOP).

Photographer: © Linda Ball.

54 I HAVE NO IDEA WHAT THIS IS EXCEPT POSSIBLY A FUSION OF ENERGY. WHEN MY PHOTOS CAME BACK FROM THE LAB, THESE WERE AMONG THEM. BEAUTIFUL COLORS!

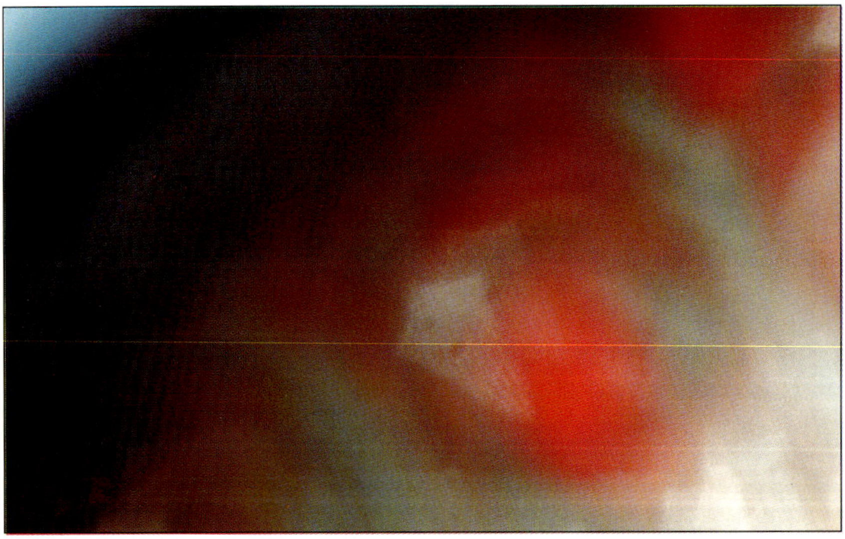

Photographer: © Linda Ball.

55 MORE FUSION OF ENERGY—NOTE THE OPAQUE WHITE FIGURES IN THE CENTER.

CHAPTER FOUR

FEAR

Most of my experiences with other beings were uplifting and filled with either awe or peace. However, on a few occasions my encounters were rather frightening. In retrospect, I believe that I had these experiences for one reason only: to allow me the opportunity to face my fear and overcome it.

The Hissing Intruder

I was enjoying a quiet evening at home when suddenly I heard our dogs barking frantically and fiercely. I rushed outside, not even taking the time to grab a sweater, even though it was a rather cold night. Gauging by the dogs' shrill barks, I knew something was very wrong. I found them gathered in a circle in a field next to our house. The hair stood up on their backs, and they were almost berserk in a frantic attack on . . . nothing . . . at least nothing I could see. What, I asked myself, could have gotten them so riled up?

Stepping a little closer, I turned in the direction they focused on, and when I did, I was electrified. I felt the chakra in my solar plexus spin erratically, my stomach churned and I became nauseated. At that moment, something approximately my height hissed loudly in my face. It was just a few feet away. My eyes could not see it, but within myself, as spirit, I instantly recognized it as something very negative. Other than the dogs, I was alone out here with this "thing" with no protection, or so I initially thought.

Indeed, my protection was with me. In an automatic reflex, I declared the ground holy and myself as a child of God. In a firm, steady voice I then demanded that the creature be gone in the name of my Father. As quickly as the words left my mouth, I heard a small "pop" in the air nearby, and the entity was gone. The dogs ceased their fierce standoff, all their back hairs again lying in place. I would like to be able to say that I pulled myself together and nonchalantly meandered back to the house. However, in honesty, I must admit that my heart pounded vehemently for quite some time. At around the same time I started finding huge three-toed prints around the ranch.

The prints were approximately fourteen inches long and averaged eight inches in width at the toes. The heels on the prints literally narrowed to a point. If it would not have been for their size, the prints could have been any reptile's footprint. I strongly suspected that those prints had been left by the hissing intruder and others like it.

❋ ❋ ❋

> The day after my fearful encounter with the hissing visitor, the messages on God continued to run through my mind. I had been told that all that is good is of God and all that is negative is of mankind's own making. Other messages emphasized that we are cocreators, creating our lives. Could it be that I had created the terrifying incident the night before? And if so, why?
>
> I was beginning to learn that we come into our lives knowing what we need to experience for our growth. Could it be that the

Photographer: © Linda Ball.

I STRONGLY SUSPECTED THAT THE HISSING INTRUDER AND OTHERS LIKE IT LEFT THESE PRINTS, WHICH WERE APPROXIMATELY FOURTEEN INCHES LONG. THEY AVERAGED ABOUT EIGHT INCHES IN WIDTH AT THE TOES AND NARROWED TO A POINT AT THE HEEL.

Photographer: © Linda Ball.

LARGE PRINT FOUND ALONGSIDE HASSAYAMPA RIVER WHILE EXPLORING WITH FRIENDS. NOTE THE SIMILARITY TO THE PRINT I FOUND ON BRADSHAW RANCH (TOP).

time had come for me to overcome fear and that I therefore subconsciously brought the encounter with the hissing intruder about? Could it be that I needed this confrontation to build my faith and to remember that my protection was within me? Perhaps. There was still much more for me to learn, and the lessons in fear were not over.

Throughout my journey, my ability to stand my ground during fearful and bizarre encounters with unknown beings was tested over and over again. These were lessons of great magnitude. Often I stood alone, with miles between me and other people. Where was I to turn? With all other options removed, I went within, to the source of my being, and called forth strength that had been hidden from my consciousness. The "negativity" vanished, but were these experiences truly negative, or did my fear create them? In time I came to realize that it was my fear that caused my negative perceptions of some of the entities I encountered. As I was able to diminish fear in my demeanor, my experiences became more and more enlightening and filled with love.

The same is applicable to everyday human relationships. Once we have learned to draw upon the energy within, which connects us to Higher Source, all encounters and relationships become nonthreatening and each person can rise to a higher level. Whenever we allow another being to pull us down into a drama of control of any sort, both individuals stagnate in their growth.

To get to the truly basic element of this, we must focus on fear. Fear is at the root of *every* negative emotion. As abstract as this might appear, if we look at it closely, we can see that anger, for example, comes about because we ultimately fear someone taking control over us. Perhaps that person's actions are altering our perspectives and assumptions which we are comfortable with. Or perhaps someone is getting away with something we don't approve of, and we fear this might affect us or those we love. Hatred is much the same, based on fear. We dislike others when we fear who they are, and we dislike what we don't understand.

When we recognize any negative emotion within we can stop and ask, "What is the fear behind this emotion?" This might appear far-fetched until we experiment with it and listen to the truth that comes from within. This is not to say that we are to suppress our emotions—on the contrary. Our emotions are very real and very valid. If we are angry, depressed, hateful, jealous or experience any other negative emotion, we should acknowledge these feelings. Bring them forth, look at them without guilt and give yourself permission to experience them. Then ask yourself what truly brought these emotions about. You see, other persons do not create anger or hate within us; rather, it is our perception of other persons and their actions that brings this about.

Yes, there are those who are very trying, but when we feel that their actions have power over us, we are allowing them to control us. What happens if we feel they have power over us? We *fear*. Therefore, fear is at the root of the emotion. When we can realize who we truly are, we can see that our worth is not—and cannot—be determined by another.

When we draw upon the energy within that connects to Higher Source, we do not need another person's energy to be complete. Once we have achieved this, all encounters and relationships become nonthreatening and each person can rise to a higher level.

Projection

Projection is the process by which one spews forth either a thought or a picture. This thought is first manifested in one's mind, then projected out into the cosmos, much as what is shown by a mechanical projector. Picture this in your mind, please.

Recall how one can place film into what you call a projector. The image is implanted on film . . . stationary. It is captured there until it is placed into the machine. The power of the machine with its various gadgets can take this stationary and stagnant image, pulse it forth through light onto a screen and create a living picture. What was once still images of people and things is now a moving picture. The captured image on film is now moving and talking.

Is that not how one's thoughts work? One can create. It begins in the heart, which is where all thoughts are germinated. Out of this heart (feelings) comes either lightness or dark. This is the base or foundation for the thought. It then goes to the mind, which creates the scenario (or storyboard, as in motion pictures). The thoughts fly fast but are still stuck on this film one calls one's mind. It formulates and becomes a solid thought or ideal. Perhaps it is very long and complicated, or maybe it is just a fleeting image . . . no difference here. It is all thought. Then the God-essence within takes this image that is formed and projects it out into one's aura, much as a projector takes an image and spews it forth . . . with what? Light! What is your God-essence? Light!

Now, as in a theater, one's aura is much like a screen, holding images, feelings and such. Think of this as your personal projection screen. What do those who enter a theater do? Why, of certainty, they sit mesmerized, watching, absorbing and becoming one with the picture and story. This, my one, is how one's aura works.

►

"But," you might say, "Others do not see my aura. It is invisible." This is not so. To the human eye it is not usually seen, but to the spiritual eye all is seen. This is going on continually without one's conscious knowledge of it. Soul sees all. Soul experiences all. You must remember this always. Yes, there are those upon your plane who consciously see auras as a natural human practice, but this message is not intended for those few, for they already know how the aura is read. Thusly, they do not need to be shown.

Now, as in previous lessons, it is remembered that *all* is put forth into one's aura. This is merely a way of telling the same thing in a manner that might be easier to remember. If one is feeling angry, resentful, bitter or hateful, please remember that you are the writer, editor, film, theater, projector and screen, all in one. Those around you are the patrons who have come to watch your movie.

CHAPTER FIVE

PRAYING FOR HELP

I came to truly comprehend the power of prayer as I traversed the rocky road of uncertainties in my research on anomalies. My messengers had advised that prayer could often be used, like a fax, for instant results. Initially, I thought that to be a bit presumptuous. Was I to understand that God was at my beck and call? That thought seemed irreverent to me at first. However, as the following two incidents show, I quickly learned that He *is* available immediately and at all times. I also learned that I had less to fear than I had imagined at times.

Danger!

Late one evening I was wandering the ranch alone. The sky was clear and the stars were magnificently bright on this cool night in early fall.

As was my habit, I was absorbing the incredible peace of the land when all of a sudden my danger-sensing radar went off and I instantly felt nauseated. Although this had happened to me before, something was different this time. Inwardly I knew that this time I was in serious trouble. To this day I don't know exactly what threatened me but the voice inside me screamed, "Danger! Danger!" I didn't even take the time to attempt to evict this energy myself but cried out, "God, send me help and send it *now*!"

Immediately, I found myself surrounded by etheric beings; they were tall, about seven feet tall. They were not in full density, so I could detect them only in a faint image as they formed a circle around me, creating a barrier to this energy that had so quickly encroached upon my perimeter. The air was filled with a serenity beyond description, and peacefulness fell upon me. I knew no harm could infiltrate my space. For a moment, I just looked around this circle of beings in amazement. In short time, my protectors literally disappeared and when they were gone, so was the danger. I will never forget that moment.

Many times we became aware of a presence that felt . . . heavenly. There are no other words to describe it. Occasionally we would detect the fragrance of roses around us, even in the dead of winter. Yet, there were no roses on the ranch, nor any other flowers for that matter, with the exception of the wild flowers that bloomed in the open field at springtime.

Followed!

Victor had taped a video of a facility in Sedona that supposedly did not exist. After he had acquired this footage, he often experienced harassment in the form of being followed, usually by white vehicles [I wrote about this in *Merging Dimensions*]. Word of this tape had filtered throughout the research community in Sedona, and I had shared the tape with several other researchers who were meeting at a home in town. Leaving the meeting at about 11 P.M., I noticed a white car parked several yards from the house. Making a mental note of this, I got into my truck and headed home.

Periodically, I glanced into my rearview mirror, and it was apparent that the white car was following me. Just as I turned onto the rough dirt road that would take me back to the ranch, I again peered into the rearview mirror. The white car was still there, a little ways behind me. I was now on high alert and accelerated my large pickup truck. The car stayed with me. There was little Moon out that night, and there were definitely no streetlights to brighten the way along the curving, bumpy road. With only my headlights to help me navigate, I now accelerated to a dangerous forty miles per hour and maneuvered the rough road, of which I knew every turn. Perhaps the strange white car would back off. It didn't.

Knowing that my options were limited, I desperately shouted out, "Jesus, help me!" I checked the rearview mirror—the car had stopped in the middle of the road, lights turned off. I slowed down and looked again. Sure enough, the car was stalled in the middle of the road. I sighed a grateful, "Thank you," and drove home to the ranch as fast as I dared.

We as humans are equipped with much more than we are aware of. We have so many abilities we never use, which is just like buying the most powerful, top-of-the-line computer and using it only to write letters. By the same token, I like to think of the wonderful messages I've received as an "owner's manual."

Prayer is a powerful lesson, and one statement in particular got my attention: the suggestion to use prayer as a tool for instant results, like a fax or an e-mail.

Prayer

Prayer . . . ah, yes. This is such a good subject. And yes, it does sound so boring. Firstly, one might ask, "Why did you not entitle this 'Meditation'?" This is done because when one meditates, one is *listening* to God or allowing light to infiltrate one's being, and when praying, one is *talking* to God.

Let us begin, shall we? Prayer itself is ever so good and ever so powerful. A great deal has been accomplished through prayer. And yet, it too has been abused beyond the function it has been intended for. Again, prayer is good. It is the *power* that is at times placed behind it that causes the abuse.

Prayer is a method by which one might send forth or emit thoughts and feelings. Prayer is transmitted out of the heart into the aura and, like a projectile, sent into the universe. The light of prayers can be very intense and bright. And yes, they are heard, but there is one thing that most do not understand. If humans are praying for an action that is against universal law, they are tying the hands of the caretakers who might act upon their request. Only if these requests are in light can they be answered immediately and as requested. Let us explain.

Perhaps one has been wronged by another and seeks some sort of revenge. This, of course, is not proper. Yes, another who has done harm will receive what you call comeuppance, but that action was already in place the moment the wrong deed was done. This is not for you or any other being on Earth to determine. Please keep in mind that this does not refer to those who require judicial action due to inflicting ►

physical harm upon others or breaking your judicial laws. Always, this is another type of instance. We speak here of those who choose to demean, inhibit or inflict emotional pain on others.

Another instance would be to plead for monetary assistance. The key word here is "plead." For, you see, monetary support is indeed your right and heritage. When you plead for this, you are saying that you do not have it or that you do not have the ability to create it in your life. In truth, it is already there if one awakens to who one truly is and in prayer gives thanks for the abundance, even if it is not visible to the eyes yet. For, you see, by accepting it and giving thanks for it with only truth in one's heart, this opens the door for the energy to begin moving. Hoping for something and knowing you already have it are two entirely different things. By pleading for something, one is saying that one does not have it and is thusly denying one's lineage and inheritance.

Another instance might be one praying for healing. Yes, by all means, release this light of healing, but pray knowing that the ability is there for the healing. Do not, I repeat, do not insist within your being that a healing is truly a miracle with slim odds of happening. No! Pray to God that you realize there is an error in this one's body, and then send forth light requesting that this one's belief in the error be dissolved. It is the belief by some humans that they have no power over the malady that many times keeps them a slave to it.

Secondly, pray that either you or another with a healing touch might come in contact with this person. There are many with healing touch walking your plane who go about their business in anonymity. They need no recognition. They have only the knowledge that they may do the Father's work. Perhaps one has prayed for a healing touch for another. The light goes forth, and then many times the message is transmitted to a worker upon your plane who then does the Father's work with a touch or a kiss upon the brow. Ever so many of these healing ones are in your hospitals, for they can apply their help so easily. We speak not necessarily of physicians with degrees in medicine (mostly healers of another type), but of what is commonly phrased as lowly employment status—perhaps a nurse's aide or a floor sweeper or a maid. Some are ever so beautiful in their light, and theirs is a great commission indeed.

Do not dismiss in entirety the element of one using disease to leave your plane. This might be that person's creation as an escape and, as such, should be honored at the time of departure. It is not always so that all should be retrieved from their malady.

The main issue to remember is that there *is* power in prayer. The key is, what power are you projecting with it? Do remember that you are always cocreator with God. Every thought and action is power. If this prayer is sent out with darkness against universal law [tarnished], then the power is diminished.

Returning to the subject of healing, if you seek healing for yourself or another, firstly realize that disease is an alien effect upon one's body. Obviously, there is an error. Ask that the error be corrected and mostly that the ill person receive wisdom. In that context, the wisdom brought forth will then correct the physical malady. As the mind goes, so goes the body. Do not discount an invisible presence creating this same thing. There is much upon your plane that is invisible to the human eye, and yet it is ever so real.

Another enormous error upon your plane (and this will ruffle ever so many) is the pleading for salvation. They want to be saved. Yes, let them pray . . . that they are saved from *themselves!* This is not meant to be funny—this is truth. For, ▶

you see, *all* are already saved. They emit from the light. It is their thought that they are disconnected that makes it so. This prayer for salvation brings one back to square one over and over again.

How many wonderful ministers upon your plane unknowingly reinforce their congregation's feeling of unworthiness over and over again? It is as if the people are kneeling in front of the Father, bowing to the ground and repeating over and over again, "I am not worthy, O Grand Master. I am not worthy." Now, tell me truth. If your earthly children fell prostrate before you every day with tears, wailing that they are not worthy, would you not hold your head and ask, "What have I done wrong?" You would have visions of them stumbling around their entire lifetime with tears flowing down their faces, saying, "I wish I could be a child to my parents but I'm not worthy. I'm worthless!" No! You would want them to claim their rightful position at the dinner table with you. You would want them to let you know when they needed a new pair of shoes in faith that you would provide this for them. You would even want them to have the confidence to ask you for the car keys from time to time. Let us take this a step further.

When they are small, they must rely upon you for everything: food, clothing, shelter and so on. They have to wait upon you to provide entertainment (perhaps a trip to Disneyland). But if parents have been wise in counseling their children to know that they have the ability to provide these things for themselves, the day will come when they will see their children walk in with new shoes bought with their own funds. They will even . . . perhaps . . . provide a meal for you! This is the ultimate goal for a parent. Why would the Creator want anything less for His children? Truly, the time is short. It is time for the children of God to stop sniveling and see ▶

themselves through the eyes of God.

When entering into prayer, always remember to ask only what is correct in universal law. Know that you have an inheritance, and see yourselves as mature children who have earned this right. Look at *your* children and recognize the welling of love within. Then place yourself in the image of the child and multiply that feeling beyond measure. Then, perhaps, you will receive an inkling of your measure. Knowing this, then proceed to pray for assistance to receive the insight to help yourselves. If truly assistance is needed, then by all means request it in the faith that it is *already done!*

Prayer is powerful. Use it properly. Know who you are, and see it as a tool, much as a fax, for instant results. Take the mystery out of it, and it will appear ever more accessible to you. This is what it is for. This is your right. Hold your head high, and go about your business (your true business) in faith and confidence, using this tool as it was intended to be used.

CHAPTER SIX

THE PORTALS

By now, encounters with invisibles and the messages I kept receiving had taught me to understand that some beings can change their vibrational level at will and therefore visit more than one dimension. As I continued my research on the Bradshaw Ranch, I was to learn that there are portals, or openings, between dimensions, which also allow access to these areas of shaped space-time continuum.

The Window

It was one of those times when I needed to take a break from anomalous life forms and reconnect with the earthly ones. So I stepped outside one evening to spend some time with my seven dogs, purposely leaving the camera in the house. My furry friends ran up to greet me, and we gathered next to the house where the huge juniper tree grew. Much paranormal activity had taken place by this tree, which was one of my favorite things on the ranch.

I sat on the grass and played with my dogs. After many hugs, pets and saying "I love you" in our own ways, I rose to return to the house. But the sight of a giant light stopped me in my tracks.

There, right before my eyes, a huge brilliant light appeared in the sky above me, as if someone in that dark expanse had turned on a giant TV. I did not see anything but the light itself, and it remained where it was for only a few seconds. Once the reality of that illumination set in, I chastised myself severely for not having the camera with me at all times. The shot of a lifetime—and it was gone. I pondered over this for several days and accepted that evidently, I was not supposed to document the light's appearance . . . or so I thought.

From then on I always brought my camera, having it ready in my hand whenever I walked the ranch. One night my preparedness paid off. The huge light appeared again in exactly the same spot. This time it was somewhat faint but still very discernable. I only had time to press the shutter release twice before the light closed, leaving me to question whether it had been real. For a long time I stood mesmerized, staring at the sky that was again studded with stars, as if nothing had happened.

Full of anticipation, I picked up the film from the photo lab, and I was stumped. Instead of a huge square of light in the night

Photographer: © Linda Bell.

THIS IS WHAT IS COMMONLY CALLED A WINDOW.

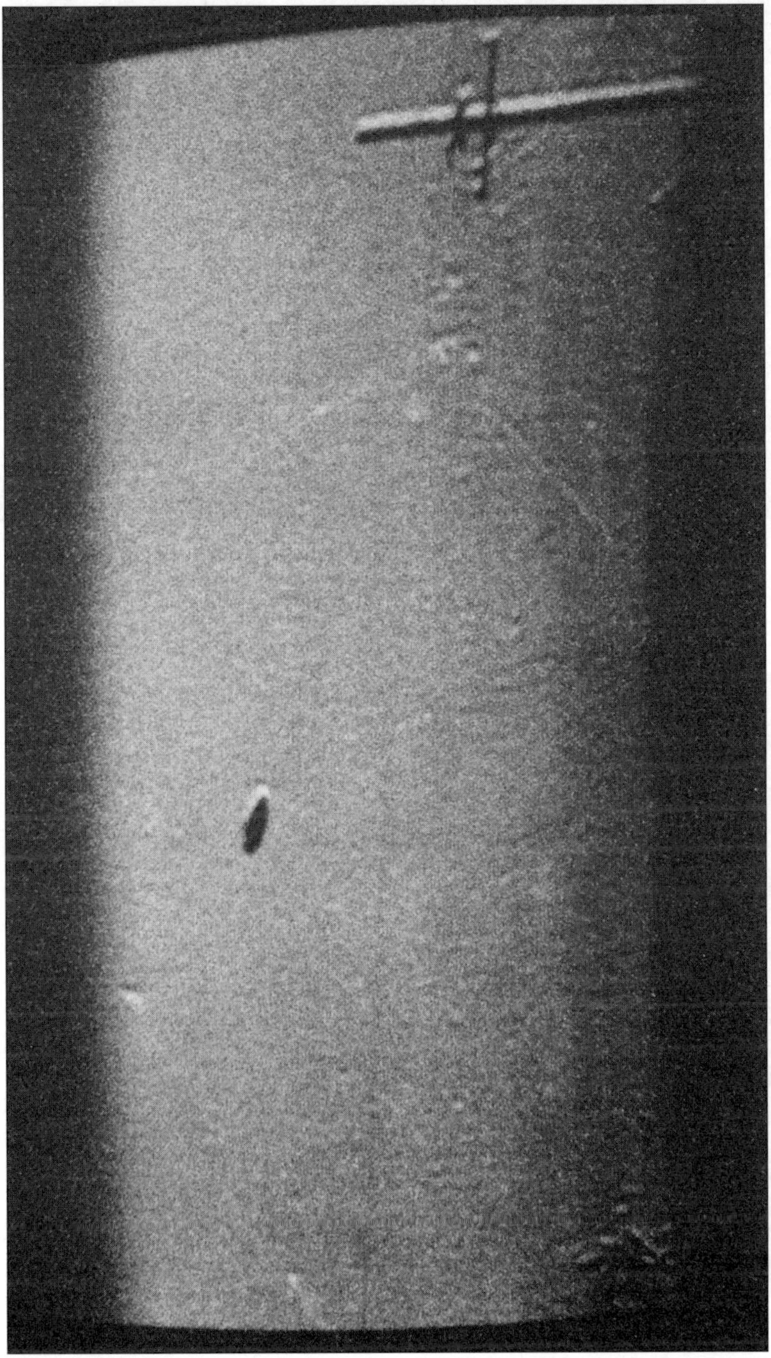

ENLARGEMENT OF THE "WINDOW" I CAPTURED ON FILM WHEN THE LARGE BOX OF LIGHT APPEARED JUST A FEW FEET ABOVE ME. NOTICE THE SEVERAL COMPONENTS: A HUMANOID FIGURE IN THE LOWER LEFT CORNER, A SAUCER-SHAPED CRAFT IN THE CENTER AND WHAT COULD BE A TELEPHONE POLE OR THE MAST OF A SAILBOAT IN THE LOWER RIGHT CORNER.

Photographer: © Linda Ball.

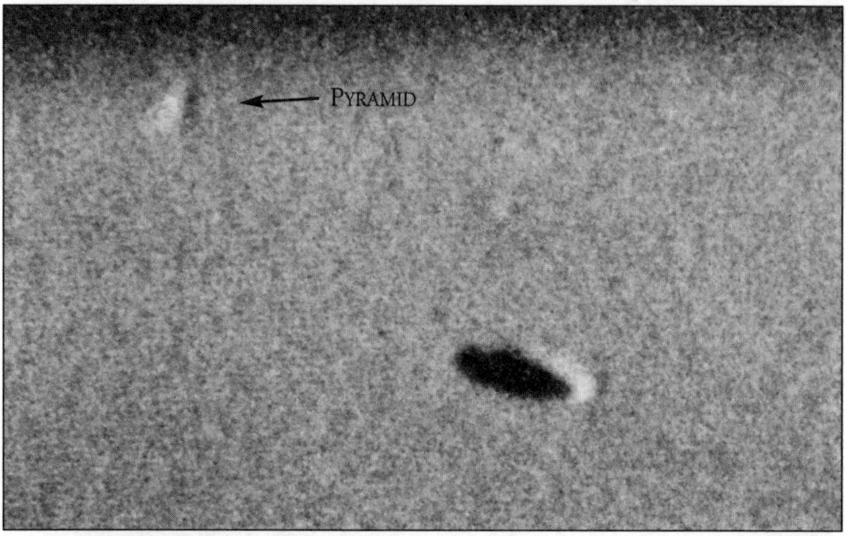

Photographer: © Linda Ball.

CLOSE-UP OF PYRAMID AND SAUCER-SHAPED CRAFT.

Photographer: © Linda Ball.

CLOSE-UP OF HUMANOID.

◀ THE LOWER LEFT CORNER OF THE PHOTO SHOWS A HUMANOID, WHO SEEMS TO HAVE SOMETHING CRADLED IN THE LEFT ARM WHILE REACHING FOR SOMETHING WITH THE RIGHT HAND. THE HUMANOID IS LOOKING TO THE LEFT.

sky as I had expected, there before me was the scene of an unfamiliar place.

The right-hand corner of the photograph shows a telephone pole or, as someone pointed out, possibly a ship's sailing mast. There were no telephone poles on the ranch; the nearest one was one mile away. In the sky, a saucer-shaped craft appears to be flying, and there is a pyramid in the background. In the lower left corner of the foreground is what I first believed to be a tree or bush. But Tom, upon closer scrutiny, noted that it also had the appearance of a humanoid, possibly carrying something in his arms. When I had the photo enlarged, it did show a humanoid.

What I had photographed that night was what is commonly termed a "window." These are areas where the veil between dimensions is very thin, thereby allowing a resident of one dimension easier access to frequencies in other dimensions. In fact, most of my encounters with beings from other worlds took place either directly beneath that opening or very close to it. I even slipped through it once and entered another dimension as I stood directly in that area.

Dinosaurs?!

Tom and I had been busy all evening photographing anomalous energies. Consequently, we both ran out of film at the same time. Tom walked to his van, which was parked approximately ten yards away, to retrieve more film, while I chose to stand there for a moment and simply watch some anomalous lights before returning to the house for additional film. I looked back at Tom, who was standing outside his van, reaching inside for his camera bag. Turning my attention back to the lights, I noticed that they seemed to be wafting in closer proximity.

Next, I experienced a slight lightheadedness—not an uncommon occurrence on that land—and right before me, I saw something that made me freeze. I looked . . . and looked again. There, approximately fifty yards away from me were two huge dinosaurs!

I held my breath, watching as these two long-necked creatures stood amidst green vegetation with leaves that looked like large palm fronds, chewing those leaves slowly. Was I looking into another dimension? No . . . both creatures turned their heads and looked at me. They could see me, which meant I was with them!

My heart pounded, and I yelled, "Tom! Bring your camera, quick!" I was frozen in my tracks and could not bring myself to move. Of all times to be out of film! There was no answer from Tom. Not wanting to take my eyes off the dinosaurs, I stayed where I was and yelled again, much louder, "Tom, come quick!" Still no response, and I became frustrated, thinking perhaps he had gone into the house. I did not want to miss this shot! Then, in an instant, the dinosaurs blinked out of sight . . . gone. I just stood there.

After what seemed like hours but was actually just a few moments, Tom came walking up to me. "Why didn't you answer when I called?" I asked. "You called?" Tom responded, "I didn't hear you." "You must have heard me," I insisted, "You were only a few feet away." Tom became very quiet and stared at me. "Linda, I was right here. If you'd called, I would have heard you."

Rather than continuing our fruitless discussion on whether or not I'd called and whether or not Tom had heard me, I told him what I had just experienced. We stared at each other in amazement. It was time for a break so, with our minds spinning, we went into the house for some hot tea.

After both of us had thrown around some theoretical possibilities, Tom came to the conclusion that he could not hear me because I was not there. He surmised that somehow I had momentarily slipped into another dimension, the same one in which these dinosaurs resided, and then just as quickly slipped back. I recalled how for a fleeting moment I had felt lightheaded and even a little "tingly" all over. However, I was not aware at all that I had ever moved or relocated. On the contrary, if someone had walked up to me while I was watching the dinosaurs and asked me where I was, I would have answered, "On my ranch, of course. Where else would I be?" It was as simple as that.

> Could slipping into another dimension be this easy? Not quite—as the message "Things to Come" (printed at the end of this chapter) points out, I did not slip through to another dimension of my own accord or heightened ability. Rather, I seemed to have been at the right place at the right time; I had been standing in the vicinity of what we now believed to be a portal.

Sounds

At times sounds filtered through a thin veil. Loud and harsh as well as low and soft, the sounds did not follow a particular pattern, nor did I hear them in one particular spot only.

Since we lived miles from anyone, there were no city or neighborhood noises, there was only the beautiful singing of the birds. Sitting at my kitchen table near an open window, I was enjoying this familiar serenity one afternoon. All of a sudden, a shot rang out, and I could hear a bullet whiz past my ear. I instantly jumped, thinking somebody had shot at me. Quickly I looked around, only to find nothing—no person, no bullet holes, no broken window and, much to my relief, no blood. I sat back down and replayed the experience in my mind. I was certain the shot had gone off in the house, but I was still alone and there did not appear to be anything amiss. I mentioned my experience to Tom Dongo and my family but decided it would be wise to say nothing to anyone else. People have been put away for less, and things were strange enough as it was.

A few weeks later, my former husband and I were having lunch in the kitchen. Without warning, a huge sheet of glass shattered right next us—only there was no sheet of glass. Both of us jumped at the tremendous noise, but again, there was nothing. I searched inside the house and outside but could not find a single piece of broken glass anywhere. I was somewhat relieved that I was not alone this time, that I had a witness, and was therefore a bit more brazen than usual in relating the incident.

Not all sounds were loud, though. Late one evening, a small group of researchers had joined Tom and myself as we were wandering about the ranch, investigating the continual phenomena. Abruptly, from out of the dark we heard chattering voices. In a higher pitch than our own, they seemed to be talking in an unearthly language. We all stood silently for a moment listening, then walked toward the area where the sounds appeared to be coming from. We found no one, and the voices soon faded. I heard the same voices again a few days later, in the morning. This time I was out by myself, walking through basically the same area where we'd heard the voices that night. Like before, the chattering voices started abruptly, speaking in the same unearthly language, and stopped after just a few moments. Although I searched the area thoroughly, I could find no visible sign of the voices' source.

I quickly learned that I could not openly share all I experienced, paranormally or spiritually, with everyone. In my enthusiasm over new revelations, I would talk about the anomalous events with a pure heart and then watch the person before me either glare angrily into my eyes or shake his or her head in pity over my "instability." Why was this?

The angry glare came from those who were firm in their belief parameters and did not want anyone upsetting this certainty, which would perhaps cause them to have to rethink their personal beliefs. Those who held pity and thought I was unstable were functioning in a pious mode, assured that anything they could not perceive themselves was nonexistent. If they were right, then I had to be wrong and, probably, crazy.

Does this make me right and them wrong? No. It was I who was in error. In time I came to understand that one must use discernment in one's dissemination of information. To overload others with information they are not yet ready to digest is only to throw a boulder into their path to awareness. What I experienced was a reality that was mine, and I was to use it to accelerate *my* awareness at *my* pace.

The particular group (or "pod") of personal friends and acquaintances I garnered over time were those with whom I could share my "far-out" experiences and encounters. We were all on the same path. As our vibrational frequencies change, more anomalous events become apparent to some, whereas they remain nonexistent to others. This will most definitely cause a rift between individuals who are walking different paths.. We are all walking the path of awareness that is vibrationally correct for us; we are neither right nor wrong. This should be honored at all times.

Things to Come

The time is near when many of you who have been called will appear to others upon your plane as either magnificent or insane. There is coming a time when there will be what you might term a "splitting off" of souls.. This splitting off will occur due to a change in vibrational frequencies in Mother Earth. Yes, as humans evolve, so do your planets. That is to say, these orbs or bodies [planets] that house you as beings will also go through a metamorphosis of a sort.

As these frequencies occur, those who are resonating at a somewhat higher level will still be what you might call ▶

"attracted" to their realm. Those who have not grown in spirit or have remained somewhat stagnant will find themselves on edge and will not know why. This is due to the fact that they are no longer in "tune" with their home, their space there upon Earth. Without empirical knowledge as a consciousness for them, they will suddenly find themselves at odds with others who have grown. This will definitely cause a rift among the peoples of Earth. This is not intentional on anyone's part; it merely is. For, you see, one can deduce one's perspective only from what one has drawn forth to that point.

Perhaps a portion of the population has come to an understanding of peace and love to the degree that they function in those ideals only. How will they appear to those who still function in the belief of power through might, such as in war and dominion or domination? Is this clearer now? This is not to say that those still functioning in the perspectives of dominion or domination are wrong. They are not, for they are doing the best they can with what they have at that given time. How might they draw forth what they have no conscious awareness of? In honesty, *their* honesty, they might see those functioning totally in light as weak individuals with no sense. This rift will not last for a great length of time due to the fact that all will resonate to the vibrational frequencies that are most compatible to their own. This brings about a severing or replacement to the proper dimensional space so that growth might continue in one's own pace. Free will . . . always free will.

Do you recall that it was stated that there are many dimensions? Thusly, as Mother Earth goes through her evolvement, so will those who reside upon her. Perhaps it is now seen how, as the phrase in your spiritual text states, two will be in a field—one will remain and another will disappear. But do not be fooled into the notion that only those of lower vibrational frequency will leave or slip into another dimension. Earth can, and will, accommodate all modalities of vibrational frequency. Those who raise their vibrational frequency at the same rate of your current dimension will remain, and others will relocate to a dimension compatible with their current understanding. Those who have escalated beyond the coming new vibrations of your dimension will be transported to a higher, more accommodating level.

These levels of vibrational change are currently in process. This accounts for the excessive stress factor in many at this time; they are on edge and know not why. The degree of their misalignment with their current dimension coincides with their degree of malfunction. The universe is a precise entity--and when there is an imbalance, it is corrected during growth phases such as the one now being experienced. This is not to be viewed as a negative, but rather as a positive step for all involved. This aligning of frequencies allows one to grow at one's own pace, taking each step in proper sequence.

All will resonate to a dimension that is compatible with their frequencies—some will be lower and some will be higher, but not lesser nor better. No, all is as it should be in this. It merely is.

Do not picture entities leaving in the manner of bodies moving to a higher or lower space. They will not move in perspective to a physical elevation. Do recall that these dimensions share the same space-time continuum. As human bodies vibrate to a certain level, they will merely merge into the other compatible dimension. The scenery might not change at *all*. They might not even be consciously aware of the occurrence.

Many will alter their dimensional abode in groups such as family, friends and so on. For, you see, these "pods" of entities are vibrating along the same frequency. Tell me, in your group of chosen friends, do you maintain company with those who function in anger, strife and control? The answer would be no to this. You choose to shun those of that nature. On the other side of this perspective, in your group of chosen friends, do you have about you those who are *totally* enlightened, such as the high masters who disappear at will or bilocate, those who can emit *only* light at all times? The answer to that would be no. You have about you those who are vibrating at your particular level; there is a camaraderie there. There is a common perspective and awareness. This same scenario holds true with most individuals upon your plane. Like attracts like. Therefore, it is highly plausible that one might go through this move in dimensions and not have a great deal of noticeable change. This is as it should be, allowing all to continue along their paths in the mode that is comfortable for them. All will continue to grow at their own pace.

Do you now see the importance of focusing only upon the light? In your current times, many are focusing on outer things, such as strife among the masses, greed, tedious daily rituals and so on. A great deal of energy is spent upon these thoughts. If they are focused on these things when a dimensional shift occurs, where are they going to find themselves *again?* Why, of certainty, on another "tour" of this duty! What one focuses upon determines one's vibrational frequency.

CHAPTER SEVEN

THIS IS NOT REALLY HAPPENING

As time passed I became more comfortable with the occurrences I was experiencing, and they started to seem less strange to me. However, a few people were unable to believe that I truly encountered such phenomena and kept taunting me.

The Doubting Thomases

As so often before, my two stepsons arrived one evening with one of their friends and began to tease me in their jovial way about my "delusions." I stood my ground and maintained that these incidents were really happening. My oldest stepson, who was twenty-four years old at the time, took a quick look at his brother and his friend, then turned back to me and said, "All right, show us!" Without a moment's hesitation, I boldly accepted the challenge: "Fine, follow me." Grabbing a powerful flashlight, I stepped through the door into the now darkened evening with the three young men trailing behind me. Once outside, I thought to myself, *What* was I thinking?! I couldn't guarantee that they would see anything unusual. Who *was* that person who'd said, Follow me? I felt that I had probably set myself up for a good dose of more teasing as I scanned the sky above us while my three doubting Thomases stood waiting impatiently.

Then I spotted it. High in the sky above us was what would appear to the untrained eye as merely a bright star. Inwardly I knew that this was not a star, but I couldn't spout to these young gentlemen that a UFO was above them. Their response would be, "Yeah, *right!*" I knew it was a long shot, but my options of producing any instantaneous phenomena were slim. One thing I had learned throughout these experiences was that they did not occur at my convenience or upon my request. "They," whoever they were, usually chose when the encounters were to occur.

Nonetheless, I lifted the high-powered flashlight, and as my two stepsons and their friend watched, I flashed three consecutive rays of light at the "star." Within seconds, a huge, brilliant beam of light shot down and totally engulfed the four of us. I stood silent—not because I was smug with the success of my mission, but because I was utterly amazed. As I absorbed what had just happened, I became aware that the three young men were shouting expletives, which I won't repeat. Before I could say a word, they raced toward their vehicle, jumped in and sped off. As a billowing cloud of dust made its way down the drive and out the gate, I looked up toward the UFO and said, "Thanks, guys."

I knew that this was not done for me. It wasn't necessary. I already knew what that light in the sky was. No, I'm convinced that this experience was custom-made for the three doubting Thomases. It was what one might call a crash course in cosmology.

Bigfoot Speaks

Another incident involved one of my stepsons and a friend of his, who also worked on the ranch. Both of these young men teased me often regarding my bold statements that a Bigfoot roamed the ranch. I'm certain they believed I had definitely gone "over the edge."

One afternoon they phoned to ask if they could hunt on the

Photographer: © Linda Ball.

This is one of the prints the Bigfoot left. It was sixteen inches long and close to eight inches wide at the toes. It had five toes, like a human foot.

Photographer: © Linda Ball.

Big Girl left this incredible full-body print of herself on sandy ground. She must have lain on her back to produce this for us. Note the one-foot ruler.

property. We had made it a policy to never allow hunting on the ranch, so I refused to give my permission. However, I suggested that they might walk across the property to hunt on the Forest Service land that surrounded the ranch. They acquiesced and arrived shortly afterward, rifles slung over their shoulders. Before they headed out, I calmly warned them that the Bigfoot—who I had named Big Girl after I realized it was a female—detested guns and that I was certain she was on the property at the time. This produced a good laugh, "Yeah, right, Linda," and they made their way out the door for their trek to the Forest Service land.

It was a quiet, fairly warm afternoon, and I had the kitchen windows wide open, allowing the breeze to filter through the house. Standing at the kitchen sink, I watched the two young men walk across the field, through the dry wash and over to a large clump of trees. All of a sudden the silence was broken by the loudest roar I had ever heard. Instantly I knew it was Big Girl, expressing her disapproval of their weapons. The sound would have made my blood run cold had I not known that she would not harm the would-be hunters. She just had a statement to make. I smiled as I waited, watching through the window. Sure enough, here they came, running as fast as their legs could carry them. Without stopping in to say goodbye, they threw their rifles into the bed of their truck and I again watched a large billowing cloud of dust race down the drive and out through the gate.

It was several days before the two young men wanted to talk about the incident, and they no longer taunted and teased me about my "delusions."

There are no UFOs!

A third incident actually backfired on me. Time and again I shared my photos with my former husband. He would smile, dismiss them and begin a different conversation. I am not criticizing him. He, like many others, would look at my photos—which showed not only anomalous lights, but also other beings who very obviously were not of this realm—and quickly dismiss them, claiming that these things did not exist. I soon learned that it is human nature to deny that which one doesn't want to see.

The boys—my stepsons and their friend—had related the bizarre experiences they'd had with me to their father. One evening he decided that this had gone too far. "Okay, if this is happening . . . prove it," he demanded. I sighed and thought, Here we go again. The odds of another UFO appearing on command were about nil in my estimation, but there was no dissuading him. Again, I grabbed the high-powered flashlight and we stepped outside. It was then that I realized that he was actually fearful, refusing to move more than ten feet away from the house. At no time did I ever wish to instill fear in another person, and I felt badly about this. I suggested we should probably just forget it for now, but he insisted he wasn't budging until I could prove to him these things actually existed.

We were standing on the east side of the house, which offered a dim view of the hills that abutted the eastern property line, approximately one hundred yards from where we stood. I was thinking to myself that this was going to be a long night. Suddenly, my husband pointed toward the south and loudly asked, "What is *that?!*" There, in plain view, was a craft, veering first toward the eastern side of our ranch, then coming straight toward us over the top of the hills. It was incredible. This wasn't a large ball of light that was coming toward us. It was a full-fledged craft, round in shape, with windows clearly visible around its perimeter. I stated, "That is a UFO." As if he hadn't heard me, he repeated, "What *is* that?!" Again I responded, "A UFO." We both watched intensely as the craft came to a halt and hovered over the tops of the hills directly in front of us. In a short time, it descended behind the ridge, where it appeared to be landing.

I quickly glanced at my husband and knew that he was terrified. Calmly, I attempted to assure him that we were safe and he

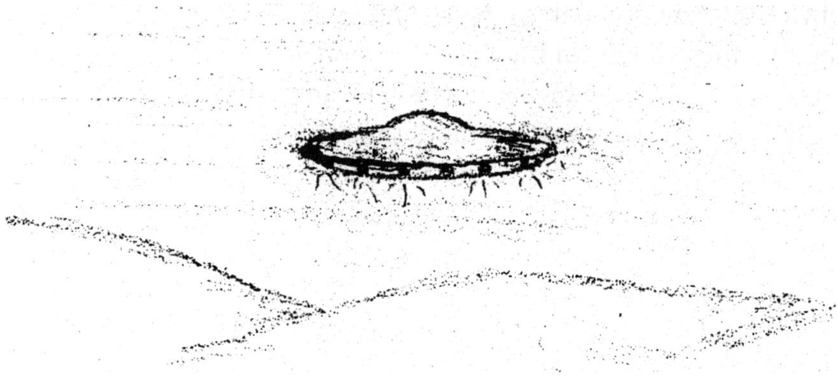

needn't worry. I don't believe he heard a word I said, as he kept staring at the spot where we had last seen the craft. He finally opened his mouth but only to yell loudly as he again pointed to the area, "*Linda!* What is *that?!*" I turned to see multitudes of light orbs cresting over the ridge and wafting onto the ranch, directly toward us.

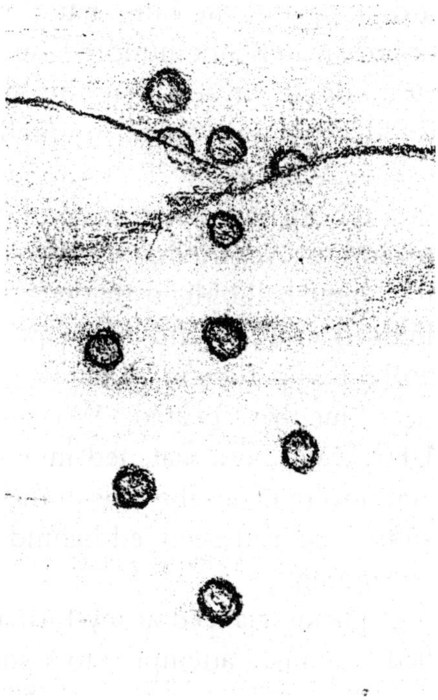

Terror had overtaken my husband; he turned on his heel and raced into the house, slamming the door behind him. I was enthralled and fascinated by this incident and dearly wished to remain outside to witness what was happening, but I was also concerned for my husband's welfare. Taking a deep breath, I walked toward the front door, placed my hand on the knob and tried to turn it. The door was locked. I knocked and asked my husband to please unlock the door and let me in. No response. I pounded harder and yelled louder, "Please open the door!" Again, no response. Hoping he hadn't locked the back door also, I walked around the house and tried that entrance. Locked. I peered into the windows and saw him sitting in a chair, refusing to let me in. As he later confessed to me, he suspected that I was one of "them" and he was therefore afraid of me. This was tragic. It took about two hours before he relented and unlocked the doors, allowing me to come in out of the cold.

I rationalized that it was not I who imposed upon him what became such a terrifying experience. He was there at his own insistence, and yet I regretted that he experienced the fright. The boys had also experienced fright initially, but in time they came to accept the incidents and even laugh about them. My husband, on the other hand, never overcame the fear. Since everything happens for a reason, I'm certain there was a reason for his experience. However, I promised myself to never again allow anyone to challenge me to give proof of the phenomena I encountered.

⁂

I knew what was truth through my experiences. Yet I also had to acknowledge that what others were saying was their truth. I learned to smile graciously when well-meaning people flung their negative opinions and doubts like darts at me, not accepting their judgment and knowing that they were entitled to their truth. Ultimately, we all were right, as we functioned in our individual phases, or generations, of our lives.

The message on death certainly held credence for me as I contended with others who, because of their own personal beliefs, attempted to discount the validity of my experiences. They let me know in no uncertain terms that I was, at the very least, delusional. In the attempt to validate their own belief structures, they felt compelled to demean my authenticity.

I would love to be able to say that this did not affect me, but that would not be the truth. For a time I accepted their judgments and strongly questioned myself and even my sanity. The photos were there to confirm my experiences, yet I still accepted the judgment of others and ended up finding myself in a downward spiral of despair. Why was this? Could it be that this was an excellent example of the power that we as humans have over each other? Death? Most certainly . . . my light began to dim, and I was becoming negative and despondent.

Looking deep within I discovered that I too had committed this crime of murdering another's light. I recalled that in years past I had discounted others' thoughts or lives, judging them to be invalid. This had come full circle now, and I could see ever so clearly how powerful and effective such actions are.

Death

Good morning, my one. I have begun this lesson backward. By this I mean I have termed the lesson "Death" so that most upon your plane might receive a picturing in their minds of the subject, but it is truly a misnomer. As we have discussed several years ago in your time, what is seen as death upon your plane is truly birth . . . birth into the realm from whence one came . . . birth of new beginnings . . . birth of return to light.

Now we will stray from birth and venture into death, true death, upon your plane. This has been disguised ever so cleverly, and perhaps it is time to look at it. There are ever so many "deaths" occurring daily. Many ones die over and over again. They do not know this. Shall we use an example?

Perchance there are ones who are happy, joyful and bright. They are connected to the Father (life source), and they have no fear, no worry. But they allow something or someone to come within their proximity, and they accept the tarnish that is thrown at them. Perhaps this other one is extremely hateful or negative, or there is an instance that, if allowed, can bring about the perception of dysfunction in one's life. Little by little, those who have accepted the errors ▶

are dying. They are becoming disconnected from their life source due to the tarnish.

This is much as one hooked to life support in your medical facilities. If this life support is damaged or not functional, the one attached will pass away either slowly or suddenly. What is the difference? There is none. To become disconnected from life source (God) is to die . . . die within. The spirit does not truly fade and leave, but it is covered over so badly that the light might no longer be emitted. So this spirit will go into hibernation until the tarnish and clutter are removed and it may shine again. This, my one, is a true death . . . death to what is real . . . death to the true life. Is this understandable?

Thusly, what is the one who purposely creates this darkness and propels it upon another? Why, this one is a conspirator to murder! Why only a conspirator? Because the one accepting this darkness is, part and parcel, as guilty. That one has also brought about this death by allowing it.

One might jest at the harshness of these statements, thinking they are a bit exaggerated. There is *no* exaggeration . . . none. One's connection to Source is truly the only lifeline to home. If humans are connected to mechanical life support in a hospital and the life support is disconnected, they do not truly "die" unless they have been disconnected from the *true* life support, God. Once the mechanism is disconnected, the *living* spirit merely goes on along its journey. It is a release. It is allowing one to go on.

Now, you might ask, "What of those who are disconnected from *true* life support when they leave this realm? Don't all go home anyway?" Yes, eventually they do, but their trek home might be a bit awkward, for they have difficulty recognizing the light they are to follow home. It is alien to them. And along the way they might encounter many things that will alter their perception or vision. Without the connection to Source, many things that they have created in their lives will return, for there is no powerful light to repel them. This is much what many call hell in your Bible. Again, do not be fooled. If you have allowed this in your life, you have truly created this as a cocreator and thusly it is very, very real. This might ruffle many, for there is a great deal of denial in this area of heaven and hell. Their denial stems from the fact that they do not see that *they* create hell. Some deny that darkness is real, believing it is a fallacy that keeps many captive. It does keep many captive, but it is truth because it has been *created.*

So, you see, true death is the diminishing of the connection to Source. It is stagnating the light, which must be moving and growing continually. It is like neglecting to water a plant. Without sustenance it withers and fades away. This brings about true devastation, leaving empty shells walking about your plane. There is death all about you.

One need not be a part of the walking graveyard. This is not what one is there for. Many, ever so many, have been sent to waken these dead and bring them back to life (Source). The time is truly short for this mission, and only if one is charged with light can one assist in the jump-start of another. You might ask how to accomplish this. As in all truth, it is ever so simple. Merely *being* light will help another. If these ones have been charged enough by your presence, they will then seek assistance for more direction to the glimmer of light of which they now catch a glimpse. Many times, merely a conversation containing one word is all that is needed.

Do you now see the tragedy we see? Many lights were sent to uplift, and in the process, they stood in the line of fire and were wounded. They did not watch closely enough for the enemy [tarnish]. It is time to stand up, brush off the dust, seek within and view the clutter. Clear it out, and completely unite with Source so that as a mature being, one might again do His work that one has chosen to do.

As the Father gave life, so shall you (as cocreator), returning life to the dead.

CHAPTER EIGHT

THE TEACHER

In Sedona I met many wonderful people and became friends with some of them. One of these friends was a gentleman who would approach me with a perplexing question regarding spiritual growth time and again, never giving me any of the answers outright but rather pointing me in the right direction, then waiting patiently as I went within to search for the answer. I have often been told, "When the student is ready, the teacher will be provided." Over the years, many teachers have crossed my path, but this friend was probably one of the greatest.

Early one evening my friend arrived at my home, and as was by then our habit, we became engrossed in yet another question-and-answer session. This lasted long into the evening, and he didn't leave until approximately 1:30 A.M.

The following day we happened to meet in a small shop in town. As we were talking, two women entered the shop and approached my friend, excitedly thanking him for having shared such an enlightening time with them the previous evening. I listened attentively as the conversation continued, revealing that these two ladies were tourists who had ventured to Sedona in search of a spiritual experience. They had been camping out in one of the canyons when my friend unexpectedly strolled into their camp, sat with them for a time and shared much enlightenment.

Now standing in front of me, they thanked him profusely for his time, emphasizing that his visit had been the highlight of their trip. I thought that the two women must surely be mistaken regarding the specific night they spoke of. I knew for certain that my friend had been with me the previous evening. As these thoughts went through my mind, my wise friend asked these ladies, "I don't wear a watch. Could you tell me approximately what time that was?" One of the women stated she was certain it was about 10:30 when he arrived at their camp, and her companion nodded in agreement. At this point I politely queried, "Are you certain it was *last* night?" "Oh yes," they exclaimed, "it was definitely last night."

My friend's appearance was very unique, so I had to dismiss the possibility that their visitor had been someone else and that they mistook my friend for him. At this point he turned to see the perplexed expression on my face and chuckled. He then turned his attention back to the women and said that he was happy he could be of service and wished them a safe journey home. They left.

I stared at this man, waiting for some explanation, but he gave none. In fact, he began another conversation with me, talking about something totally different. This was too bizarre, and I could not dismiss it. "Okay," I said, "if you were at my house until 1:30, how could you have been in their camp at 10:30?!" He just calmly shrugged his shoulders and asked, "How do *you* think that happened?"

In all the time I spent with him during the following months, he never gave an explanation nor did he bring the subject up again. It was up to me to come to the realization that he had bilocated. This man was a master and as such chose not to proclaim his abilities. He merely went about, sharing his light with whoever was in need of it. He did not desire notoriety, only an ability to assist others. For this reason, I do not give his name.

Several months after that incident he quietly left town, telling no one of his destination.

Twins, and More

Ever so many comprehend that when one "dies," as you call it, one's self, as spirit, leaves the body and carries on. If this were possible, then why would it not be possible to have twins of oneself elsewhere? By this we mean that the twin is not necessarily always in human body but is a split-off of the spirit, such as twins are a split-off of the embryo while in the womb. Do you recall when we stated that everything is the same in the universe? So one can look at one's life there and understand that whatever is possible there is possible in *all* forms of life throughout the cosmos. There are twin planets, there are twin human forms, there are twin aspects of the spirit. We shall take this to another level.

Does not the embryo split off into several humans while in the womb? Most certainly. There are triplets, quadruplets, quintuplets, sextuplets and so on. The picture is now coming into focus. One spirit might be experiencing several factions of itself in several forms at the same time, but it is done in the form of a dream. This brings clearer understanding to the issue of bilocation. Reports are given for all time of masters appearing in two places at the same time.

Now let us clarify something else, if we may. This does not mean that your existence there is unreal. It is very real and very necessary. You are very real and very necessary. Your experiences are real, your emotions are real. When the human body is cut, it bleeds. Your lows and highs are very much real, for *you* are real. By using the term "dream," we are saying that these dramas being played out are being recalled and experienced by the base faction of spirit just as you are experiencing them. ["Base faction" will be explained further on in the message.]

►

Before we go on in this issue, we would like to sum up this information so it remains clear. There are many facets and forms of the spirit called *you*. What you are currently experiencing in your human form is but *one* of these facets. As you live out your life there, messages are received by another facet of you, which is a base of you as spirit. Being multifaceted, one might be experiencing many levels or tiers of experiences at the same time, even though while in your form there on Earth you recall and consciously experience only your earthly life. This is as it must be, but always remember that the base *you* is absorbing all experiences and facets that you as a split-off spirit are living. This might all be on Earth or, as in most cases, in other dimensions or on other planets.

We would now like to delve further into the issue of one as spirit, if we may. As we mentioned, spirit is multifaceted and, as such, is capable of taking on varied forms. When this is done, spirit can travel many places. Do you recall the many, many photographs you've acquired in your search for truth? Indeed! This, our one, is a picturing of the events where spirit has broken through the barrier of dimensions many times. At times it will appear in a wispy form; at other times it will be in full form but will not be viewable by the human eye.

As you discovered, the "eye" of a camera is capable of perceiving and duplicating the image that is invisible to the naked eye but is indeed truly there. When one is in full beingness one might consciously take on other forms and travel anywhere merely at the instant of a thought process. There is no time as you know it, but we will expound further on this subject at another time. When one is aware and knowing of the absence of time, one can thusly manifest oneself to any place or time (as humans gauge) as the mere thought occurs. The ▶

Blue Man, as you call him, was indeed an example of this. Our one, we have been working with you for quite some time to bring about this awareness.

All of life is an electrical unit, vibrating at certain decibels, which holds mass form together. This life form and its electrical vibration are in tune with the wonderful entity you call Mother Earth. Synchronicity is always in play. For most, with their current understanding, vibrational level is at one setting to accommodate their experiences on Earth. As one arrives at more knowledge and understanding, the vibrational setting multiplies (again, multifaceted), allowing one to alter frequency and thusly become accommodating for other electromagnetic frequencies in other places. These are the ones you call masters. They are in full conscious knowledge of their beingness and thusly change frequency at will.

Some of you who are outwardly unaware of this ability within yourselves receive reports that you've been seen in two places at once or suddenly have memories of being somewhere when logically you know you did not leave. Why is this? How can this happen? We will tell you.

Again, we revert back to base spirit. Base spirit has all knowledge and all capability. At times the call is given by the base *you* to have this experience. Why is this? Because it is time. Nonetheless, the ability is there for many. Why is this necessary? It is only when one comes to the full knowingness of one's beingness that one can "cancel," if one wishes, the need for all exercises and regimentations one is experiencing while in one's dream on Earth. Please do not misunderstand when we always refer to Earth. This is the case on other planets also. We merely use Earth as a reference due to the fact that this is where you reside.

As one reads further, it will behoove one to remember that *all* (all life and all experiences) is multifaceted. This will allow ▶

understanding to come more readily. For a short time, erase all programming that declares only one of anything. Humor us for a time and visualize every experience and all existence as split into multifaceted forms.

CHAPTER NINE

TIME

It was the morning after an unusually eventful night. A UFO sighting and an encounter with Grays (“Grays” on page 40) had brought Victor, his lady friend and her then seven-year-old daughter from the house on the north end of the ranch to the main building. We spent the remainder of the long night together, and by early morning, we ventured out to see if our nightly visitors had left any tracks behind.

The four of us slowly made our way to a dry wash not far from the house, then descended into the wash. My son went in one direction, the rest of us wandered off in the other, and we were soon separated by several yards.

“Mom! There’s a dinosaur in the wash!” I suddenly heard Victor’s voice bellow out. We ran to join him as fast as we could, and the seven-year-old girl was the first to get there. She chimed in loudly and excitedly, “Mommy! There! There, a dinosaur!” The young mother and I arrived just in time to see what appeared to be a huge tail scurrying into the heavy, tall brush farther down the wash. Both Victor and the girl had seen the creature, and their descriptions matched exactly: It was approximately five feet tall, stood erect on both hind feet and was somewhat of an earthen color, what one would call a light, dusty brown. Once the dinosaur was gone, we started looking for tracks. Unfortunately, the rocks and boulders at the bottom of the wash did not show any imprints the dinosaur might have left.

I tried to gather my wits about me and then rationalized that it must surely have been a species I had read about called the Reptilians. I mentioned this to Victor, and he gave me a blank look, asking, "What's a Reptilian?" I explained that some believed that a species of humanoids from another place exists that closely resembles lizards. After all my son had experienced up to that point, this idea seemed plausible to him. However, other events made me less certain we'd seen a Reptilian. After all, I had experienced the other dinosaur escapade near the house . . .

My experiences and other messages I'd received had prepared me for the message on time. However, as I already mentioned, discernment is very important when gauging how much information is beneficial to another's growth and understanding. To overload others with knowledge that is far beyond their comprehension will only lead to them veering off their path. The following message could fall within the category of "overload." If this message seems preposterous, unbelievable or just plain crazy to you, then simply label it as such and go on. Dismiss it from your thoughts. The words in this book are meant for many; take what you need and leave the rest.

Time

Time, as we have mentioned, does not truly exist. This is one of the most difficult aspects for mankind to comprehend due to the fact that "time" is a basis for all things upon the realm you reside in. There is "yesterday," "today" and "tomorrow." All daily experiences function to the hands of a clock. The Sun rises at one "time" and the Moon at another. One does not perceive oneself as existing in yesterday again. One is now in today. The scenario goes on and on.

This framework of time is indeed good for those who are not yet ready to come into full beingness in the form of a master. This would, as you call it, overload their circuits in their current understanding. As you have stated, this would be parallel to placing a boulder upon their path of awareness. They would see this boulder as too tedious to overcome and therefore turn back upon their path.

For those who have chosen and earned their graduation into mastery, the issue of time must be dealt with. It is a great millstone around one's neck in one's endeavor to forge ahead. Time holds one captive to the immediate surroundings, does it not? Perhaps one would wake and state, "This is Tuesday, I go to work, I come home, I go to bed at 10:00," and on and on. Time keeps one on the treadmill of "today." This focus on time prevents one from focusing on anything else in the form of the total reality of existence. One thing to remember is that all is happening at the same time. It is mankind's inability to comprehend this that makes time a necessity.

We tell you truth. If one chooses, one can step through into another dimension and reexperience perhaps your Civil War. "Aha!" you think, "The dinosaurs!" Indeed. Do you, in logic, perceive dinosaurs to be in existence any longer upon your land? Nay! Those are of the "past," and yet you momentarily saw them alive and well. Yes, yes, we understand your questioning. Yes, perhaps you subconsciously "created" this experience for your growth. In most instances this would be true. But do understand that as one grows toward one's goal of merging with–and understanding of–all, another phase takes place, and that is the emergence into mastery. In this phase, one no longer "creates" experiences for growth; one enters creations (experiences) for others' growth. Is this understandable? Again, while on the path of initial growth, experiences are created to bring one to the ultimate understanding that one can outgrow and has outgrown this negativity. Once this is outgrown, one then chooses to "see" and experience the reality, the whole picture, in the effort to bring others to this understanding.

We wish to return to the essence of this message of time. Picture, if you will, those who might be in a theater, watching a movie. Perhaps this movie is picturing a "past" time, one hundred or more years ago. They are absorbed in this story, and yet if they look around themselves, they will see that they are indeed not in that "time." They are "watching" that time and are existing in a modern theater. A master sees life in your realm as much the same. It is merely a movie . . . or perhaps a dream, hmmm? With this clarified, we will go on.

We shall break this equation down to another level. Do recall that we've made the statement that humans create their lives. In this aspect, could it be possible that even Earth has been created for one's experiences? Yes, God, as base spirit, is mentioned as creating the universe. But as a faction of this spirit, could it not be possible that even the current "knowledge" of Earth, the outer cosmos and all of its life is another part of the unreality played out in one's growth? This is quite a scenario to think about.

One, you have yet much to learn and are merely peeking through the door of more truth. At this point, some of these aspects might appear as a dichotomy, superseding the boundaries of human logic. This is as it is. Perhaps it is "time" to open the door a bit wider. Time, our one, is real only in the measurements of one's proximity to these doors. How "long" will it take to open them? But once they're opened, time will be recognized as nonexistent due to the fact that knowledge will then be instantaneous. What we have given you is very advanced and more need not be said. It will take some "time" to absorb these possibilities.

SECTION II

FILMING THE EVENTS

After the release of *Merging Dimensions,* a great interest in the material shared in the book brought about a phone call from Scott Catamas, the producer of *Paranormal Borderline*, which was broadcast on a major network. He asked if it would be permissible for his film crew to come to the ranch and film a segment for the program. Tom and I discussed this and agreed. I had never been on television before, so I was a bit apprehensive of the whole ordeal. But I thought, What the heck—a new experience.

Scott and his crew arrived early and advised us that they would be staying late because they wanted to acquire both daytime and nighttime footage. It was his greatest desire to be able to catch some of the phenomena on film for the show, so he asked if I could try to contact these beings telepathically, asking them to appear in some form. I breathed a deep sigh and told him that I couldn't guarantee anything. "These things normally do not occur for our convenience," I explained. However, since he was such a nice man and had been very polite when he asked, I agreed that I would try but I could not promise anything.

While the film crew was setting up the equipment, I went to a secluded room and telepathically asked for a "special" appearance that night. My guides responded with the message that beings would appear, albeit not in full form, since it was not yet time for them to be thus disclosed to the mass of the public. Still, something would occur that would be acceptable as a form of proof that the phenomena really were occurring. This was very interesting. When I went back outside, I didn't mention the promise I'd been given but merely told Scott that I had done what he had asked. We would wait and see if anything happened. Scott explained to me that in all of the episodes they had filmed thus far, he had yet to be privileged with seeing an incident himself.

Inwardly I hoped my guides would keep their promise. After years of receiving messages I had learned that it was a rare occasion when I received a promise of anything from my messengers, and I had learned that they never lied. But I was concerned about my

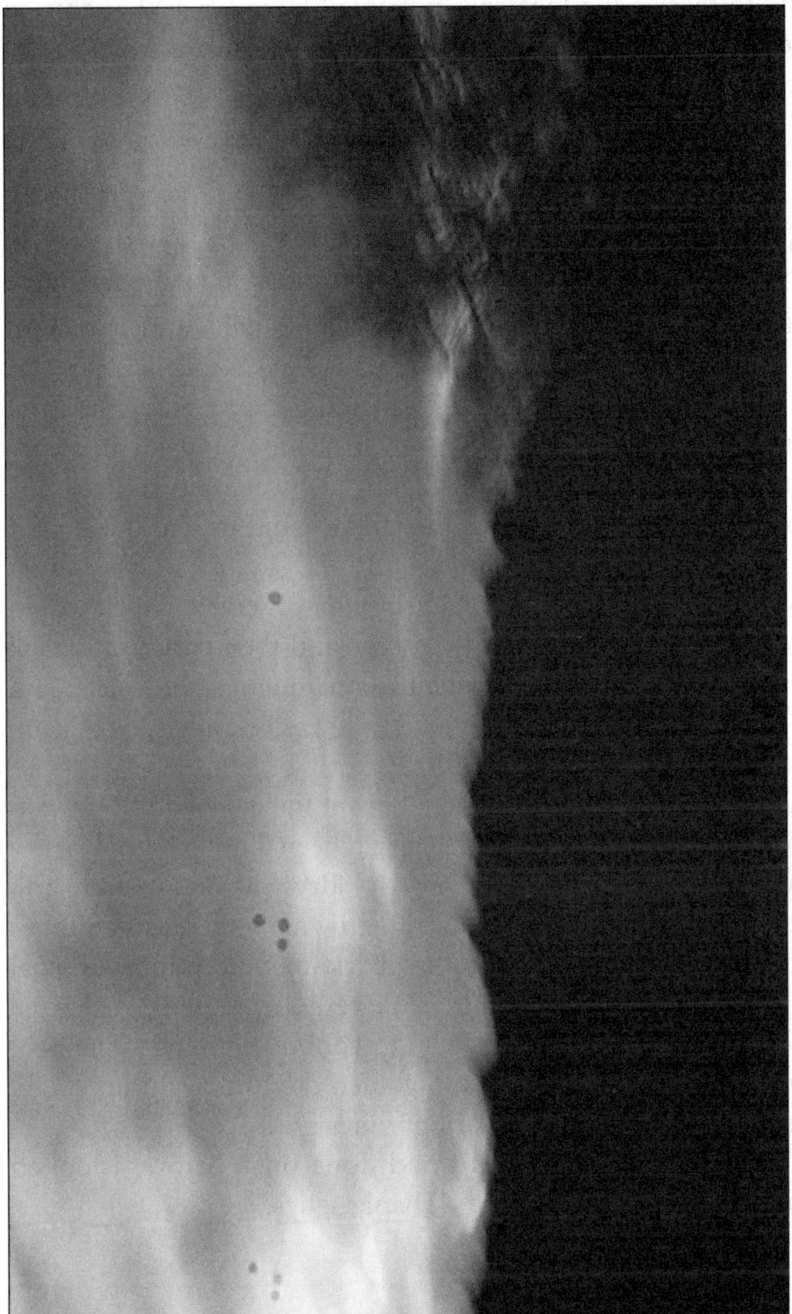

GOLDEN BALLS OF LIGHT THAT APPEARED WHILE I WAS ENACTING A PHOTO SESSION FOR *PARANORMAL BORDERLINE.*

Photographer: © *Linda Ball.*

ability to receive the messages untainted by my own thoughts or hopes. To this day I check myself inwardly to ensure that I do not alter my guides' messages with my own thoughts.

The filming went well during the early hours as we re-created some of the scenes that were in the book. Tom and I were interviewed as were my son and others who resided on the ranch, along with Brian and Tina, two researchers who had spent many years on UFO phenomena. Then darkness came and it seemed as if electricity was in the air. The film crew was in hopeful anticipation of something, anything, to catch on film.

I had kept the promise of an impending event secret, had not even told Tom about it. For a time we all stood outside in a spot where we often saw anomalous lights, just watching and waiting. Tom and I had been scanning the land around us and the sky for a while when he calmly pointed up to the sky toward the south. There was the small light we had so often observed, which would rise from the horizon, hover for a time and then either sink back down below the horizon or instantly blink out of sight. Since Tom and I were familiar with this "whatever it was," he advised the cameraman to begin filming the light.

Although this was not the major event the crew had been waiting for, the cameraman obliged. He had been filming for only a few moments when the light suddenly exploded with an intensely brilliant gold color. It was magnificent, growing to at least ten times its original size and then imploding back upon itself to its original size. I heard Scott yell, "Gold! We've got the gold!" Then he quickly instructed the cameraman to continue filming. The light again pulsed to a huge, brilliant, golden orb and again imploded upon itself, this time disappearing from sight.

The crew was elated. As I had done once before, I looked toward the sky and softly said, "Thanks, guys."

SECTION III

MESSAGES

When the transmissions first began, I received just tidbits of information—perhaps one sentence or two at a time—that was relevant to what I was experiencing. As is required for a toddler, I was fed only what I could really absorb. As time went by the information grew and filled what often seemed like reams of paper with the nourishment for my growth.

In 1985 I had experienced the death of my fourteen-year-old son, which left me in an emotional tailspin, and I didn't believe I could pull out of it. I was living alone at the time and often found myself in solitude during those long days and nights as I journeyed through the depths of grief, anguish and despair. Quite frankly, if it had not been for the love of my then eighteen-year-old other son, I would not have wished to go on.

It does not always take something as drastic as the loss of a child to open one to guidance. Whatever our circumstances are, there is a turning point, a junction in our path, that brings us to the time when we are willing to hear.

CHAPTER TEN

IN THE BEGINNING

The following pages contain but a small fraction of the messages I received during the first years of my travels down the path of spiritual learning. The subjects in these messages were many, and similar topics were often touched upon in different ways.

My elementary lessons had one basic theme, love—love for God, others and myself. And I was taught that it was imperative to continually reach within to my reservoir of strength.

I began meditating, and it was then that the messages came pouring in, filled with such wisdom and knowledge of things I had previously known nothing about—at least I thought I hadn't known about them. In time I came to understand that this knowledge is accessible to us all. It is there all along. As my messengers so clearly stated, "There is nothing to seek, only something to claim." That one small sentence, comprised of a mere nine words, spoke volumes to me.

Simplicity

Please do not misconstrue the statements regarding physicians in the following message. Many times these messages are meant for those who have come to the point in their growth where they are capable of creating a healing within themselves. Most upon our plane have yet to achieve this goal. A physician is necessary for most, and it would be very detrimental to eliminate the medical profession prior to one's full awareness.

When I received this message on simplicity, I thought, Easy for you to say! How can I simplify my thoughts when I'm in the middle of this mystery? In time I came to discover that only simplicity could clear my path to discovery. As I pondered the phenomena, which appeared to engulf me more and more, I was allowing old thought forms and patterns to tarnish what was readily apparent by attempting to categorize the unknown within my limited perceptions. I did not achieve simplicity of thought overnight and only through many defeated attempts at solving these mysteries did I finally submit to clearing out all preconceived notions of what this world is about. I had to start with a clean slate. It was only when I could release my ego, admitting that I knew very little, that answers began to filter in.

I believe this aptly applies not only to mysterious phenomena, but to all life. When I began to apply the theory of simplicity in my everyday life, a great burden was lifted. I discovered that I had been my own worst enemy, insisting on complicating that which was in truth very simple.

The greatest detriment to one's awakening is overcomplexity. As a resident of planet Earth, it is often—or should we say, most often—that one is trained in the ways of complexity. This is the way of life upon your plane. It transmits from the need of most humans to feel great accomplishment in their endeavors, and if it has been a great complexity to conquer, they are to others indeed great solvers of puzzles, are they not? This is not a criticism but merely an observation of the main barrier to seeing truth.

Let us continue. The basis of reality in *all* aspects is simplicity. Once one can come to this realization, one has been freed of the mind-boggling barriers constructed to keep one at arm's length from freedom. To keep the lesson itself from being complex, we will begin with common scenarios. ▶

The medical profession upon your plane is wondrous indeed and is filled with great entities who receive instruction from those of us watching. Mostly, this is not known to the receiver, but nonetheless, it is done. At present, it is necessary to send forth information in a way that is acceptable to the human population in general; therefore, it is mixed with complex puzzles and answers. One might stew over a solution to a disease for months or years and then, *voilà!* The truth breaks through at last . . . the answer. This, in truth, is not necessary in reality, but upon your plane it has been a necessity for understanding . . . or as your term reflects, comprehension.

This has been done in good time, but as in your individual cases, it is time for a rebirth of your planet in general. This encompasses many factions, and it is time to awaken to the reality of simplification.

Let us use an example of awareness simplification. Many upon your plane have meditated until their heads want to burst, in an effort to receive direction and enlightenment; is this not truth? Of certainty. This has not been wrong in any way. Meditation and prayer have indeed uplifted the planet by bringing light upon your plane. These practices have sent messages forth, which in turn called light to them. This is good. What I wish to explain is the fact that long, tedious rituals are not truly necessary for the calling forth of light and wisdom.

Firstly, all light and wisdom are already embedded within each one. Without the knowledge of how to open that well of truth within oneself, it has been necessary to call forth light to receive the power that generates the awakening of this source within. Is this understandable? Indeed. Therefore, what I say is that the deed is accomplished, but the long route is taken to achieve the goal.

▶

Many upon your plane have the perception that it is sinful to reach within because they feel they are omitting God from the process. This is not truth, for the God-essence is and always will be ensconced within. It is much like needing to buy something at the market that is two doors down. They step out the door and, forgetting that they can walk there, get into a vehicle, drive around the block and enter the parking lot of the market. They still get there and the deed is accomplished, but the vehicle was not truly necessary and the trip could have been accomplished much sooner had they remembered they could walk two doors down. This is the same thing. Your vehicles [bodies] have been used for so long that most have forgotten that their legs [spirit] are very useful and that the market [God] is ever so close. Is this understandable?

There is nothing wrong with reaching directly within and receiving what is *already* there . . . it is, has always been and forever will be. The only difference is that one forgets this. This now becomes a matter of realizing that this existence is not only of the past, but is inclusive of the *Now,* which one is blinded from. It is a matter of reaching in and pulling out an inheritance of your higher self.

"Aha," you might mutter, "You are saying that I am God. I find this questionable." No, my one, this is not what is being said. Your higher self is the "essence" of God. You are a parallel essence of this higher self, thereby making you a child of God. The only difference is the fact that this higher self has instantaneous access and does not need the long route that you have needed up to now . . . or felt you needed.

When one reaches within, *knowing* that one has this wisdom, one can therefore create many wondrous things for not only oneself, but for all around one. Do you remember the lesson of all energy going into the auras [the message on Projection]? How wonderful it is to emit this instantaneously.

At no time is one disconnected from God in this process. Indeed, one is even closer, for one is using the God-given abilities to do His work on Earth. Remember, only you can tarnish or cover over this connection to God-source if this is used improperly.

Returning to the comparison in your medical profession, recall now in your mind the ones who are called miracle healers upon your plane. Yes, some are not, in truth, using their power properly, and this will be dealt with in proper time. But also, there are ever so many who are not famous, yet they go about healing others with a touch of their hands. Now, the person who is healed could have gone to the hospital and eventually been healed through either surgery or medication. This is truth by the long route. But the person can receive the same healing instantaneously by receiving the touch of one who has a true awareness of the God within, who knows no error and can overcome all. What is illness? It might be a result of tarnished power in one's thoughts, or most often it is many decades of the illusion that one is powerless over this dark malady. Now call forth the information of previous lessons where it is taught that all power is from God. If one cannot comprehend the aspect that light can overcome this tarnished malady, then perhaps another might, with the knowing within, send forth this power to overcome and remove the disease [dark tarnish]. This is truly a matter of physics.

This again brings about the matter of simplicity. If one could only acknowledge at *all* times that light (God) is all power, there would never be a doubt that one was not helpless nor hopeless to any factor upon your plane.

Taking simplicity to its basest form, one must know that there is only *one* power in existence . . . only one. That is light, God. There is only one alteration to this power, which ▶

is darkness. Only disconnecting from the light can alter its effect, bringing about this darkness. Where there is an absence of light, there is darkness. The light is ever more powerful but in its absence the darkness finds an abode. Simplicity. There are multitudes of levels at which one can see or experience the power of light but again, there is only one power.

So, you see, when they come to you and say, "Oh, I know for a fact that there is evil. There is a Satan who wreaks havoc upon mankind, bringing about destruction," please know for certain that they are telling you truth. For, you see, this darkness has been created. It has been given life; therefore, it exists.

Now, as in the text of your Bible, does it not say that God created all, even Lucifer? Lucifer was indeed the most beautiful of the angels. It was Lucifer's *thinking* that made him dark, that got him thrown out of heaven (disconnected from the light). One's thinking does indeed create this demon in reality. As creator of this demon, one will be visited often by the dark child one created. Do your children not return home often? Do they not feel comfortable there? The difference here is that your children were created in light and this demon was created by tarnished thoughts.

Simplicity . . . take every aspect in your life—family, job, talents, spirituality—and see which power you have given it. If it is tarnished at all, remove the darkness immediately and return it to the initial, only true source, God. When this is done, the process is immediate. You have transposed any darkness in your aura to light, which immediately draws the light back to you and repels any darkness.

In reference to one's spirituality, this can be, as you might say, an awesome experience. Pull forth any and all thoughts of yourself. In truth, are there *any* areas in which you see ▶

yourself as anything but a child of God? Is there any small nook or cranny where a dark thought of yourself might lurk? If there is, it is tarnished and therefore diminishing your light, your power. So many say, "I know I'm not perfect, but I try ever so hard. I am going to change my actions and become a better person." This is backward. Try simplicity. If all thoughts are purged and the image is reviewed, one can see many areas of thought that *cause* the actions. If the thoughts are changed, the wrongful action immediately disappears. It no longer has a place to reside. It is repelled by the light.

Do not see this as encouraging pious thinking of oneself. Simply, pious thinking is tarnished thinking. What is meant here is encouragement to see oneself and all others as beautiful, wondrous beings who are tangled up in a maze of backward thinking that has temporarily diminished one's light. If one can see and eliminate this tarnish, then the light emitting from one's aura will direct others toward the path of truth . . . of simplicity.

To achieve this simplicity is very simple, as is all truth. Take an inventory of your image and determine that all deadwood must be cleared out. Deadwood is anything that clutters your thoughts and takes them away from the knowledge that there is only one true power of which you are a part. Just sweep the deadwood away, leaving a clean house for the God-light to shine within. In simplicity you will find that this light has been desperately trying to break through. Become familiar. Become very close to this light, for it is the essence of your being. As you become close to it, you will find a connection to God that will be beyond your greatest experiences.

You are loved ever so dearly.

Generations

The message on "generations" was so appropriate as I stumbled through each stage of growth brought about by one revelation after another. I had been on the ranch for seven years, and it was easy to look back and see that I was far from the person who first stepped foot on that land. My perceptions and demeanor had definitely been altered.

These generations that we speak of, my one, are those that one individually lives through during one's life span upon Earth. Each one thinks of generations as separate lifetimes experienced by separate individuals. This is so, but there are also generations in *each* individual lifetime. Let us begin with this in mind.

As a soul or entity, each one leaves home with the anticipation of growth, learning and upliftment of more than oneself. Within the growth of each one comes upliftment and acceleration of those around him or her. The growth is shown in electrical energy, which emanates from within and flows out into the aura. So, you see, whether one word is said or not, the light continues to flow out and bring more light to others.

Now, you might ask, how does this tie in with "generations"? This is done, my one, as a step up, you might say, in one's consciousness. Each step up is a generation in one's lifetime. Let us phrase it in terms of your experience: The entity entering in a birth might be seen as the great-grandfather of the entity that will be leaving your plane when all work is done. Thusly, the infant brings in a certain amount of awareness and knowledge. But as this entity walks the path of life, each rock that is stumbled over in the name of learning will bring that one to another point of awareness, which is, in truth, another birth. This new birth is the new generation of this *same* entity. When one has experienced these birth pangs ▶

and brought forth a new awareness, it should be a celebration as is each physical birth upon your plane.

Then, for a time, the new generation of the same entity will enjoy its infanthood, shall we say. It will smile, coo and be coddled. Then it will tire of the limitations and attempt crawling, which will (and always does) bring bumps and bruises. In spite of this, try to stop this little one from crawling. It cannot be done. The curiosity is so grand and the drive is so strong. So it will survive the lumps and bumps until it is ready to walk. The entity then, having survived the birth pangs, enters into the walking stage—another birth. Can you now see how one entity can experience many generations?

Each stage of growth is a new birth, which brings with it a new personality. Are you, in entirety, the same one who forged through the birth canal? Of certainty, you are not. That little being had a life that is far from yours now, did it not? As in separate generations, there is still the family resemblance—the same eyes, the same complexion and so forth. But also as in separate generations, there is a different agenda than the one your grandparents had for their lives. They are the same, and yet they are different. Do you now see the similarity? You are not entirely the same one who birthed, and yet the similarities are still there and are carried on.

Shall we take this a step further? Would you *want* to have the same agenda for your life that your grandparents did? Very few would answer yes to this question. Everything around you has changed, and you would feel very antiquated indeed, should you remain stagnant. It is much an occasion for rejoicing when a new little being is brought into the family. This is truly how you should see each birth in your life . . . each level . . . each new personality. The original gene still flows through, and yet if constantly nurtured by the light of ▶

God, each time it is improved.

There are yet more births to come, and each one will be glorious. Do not cling to the rattles and teddy bears of infanthood, which will keep you in the time warp of your latest birth. Pull yourself up, crawl, walk and then run with great strides.

Your Bible tells you to be thankful for your adversity. What it did not do is complete the original thought. It was meant as thus: Be thankful for each adversity, for it is a step to new birth. Do you now see how the statement in this same liturgy ties in with the one that says, "Ye must be born again"? Unfortunately, those of your Christendom have been misled to a degree. They teach that they must merely say a few words and they are instantly reborn. The surrendering to light is very grand indeed, but to experience the true rebirth, one must walk the path of stones with perseverance and know that these birth pangs are what bring the true new birth. This is not to be construed as a dichotomy of the previous lesson that simplicity will eliminate the long route to spiritual enlightenment. This statement is meant for those who reach an awareness of growth following many rebirths and can obtain simplicity at that time.

The ultimate agenda is to reach the pinnacle of unnecessary rebirth. This is what silently drives one from birth to birth, much as a salmon swims upstream. This goal is inevitable but is not reached as early as many assume. So many upon your plane declare that they are past the point of requiring new lessons. They are "enlightened." This is admirable thinking, and yet the statement itself avows new lessons to be learned. For, you see, one who needs no new births has this knowing without a need to proclaim. Yes, some are closer to that goal than others, but all are still learning. All are beautiful children in our eyes.

▶

How you love those little bundles you've birthed and what joy you receive in watching their steps of growth! This is how you are seen from others here . . . as so beautiful, so lovable and so cherished. If only all could see themselves through God-eyes. The journey through generations would be walked along the path of gratefulness rather than dread or regret, rather than anger, resentfulness, disheartenment and sadness. Look again in the mirror, my one, and see what we see. Experience what we experience when we see you. That is joy unending.

May your journey be uplifting and joyful.

Martyrdom

The message on "martyrdom" stirred up many thoughts about myself as a parent. Had I been guilty of this? Reluctantly, I had to admit that, to a degree, I had. The barbs dug deep as I recalled times when I pressured my son to be whatever I believed was right for him. Those issues had given rise to great conflict, and the message brought forth a clear picture of the underlying cause. I flogged myself mentally, but most importantly, I asked my son's forgiveness, admitting that I had been in error. Being the wonderful person he is, he immediately dismissed any guilt on my part and assured me that I was a great mom, but the smile on his face told me how appreciative he was that I was able to see his pain. From that point on we became very close, and I am ever so grateful for the wise words, which had initially hurt so much.

Ah yes, martyrdom, my one. How one loves to dangle one's value and suffering before others. This has a basis, to a great degree, in the biblical text that states that those who die as martyrs for Christ will receive many crowns. How misinterpreted this has become.

Firstly, let us look at the complexity of the message against the statement from this same text that says thou shalt not be a braggart, or that one should fast and pray in silence lest one might be using one's spirituality as a means of praise or approval from others. But you might state that martyrdom is meant as willing to die for the cause or belief in God. Let me tell you truth.

Martyrdom was not intended to mean this, and the scripture has been sorely mistranslated, thusly being misinterpreted. If one but looks deeper, one might find ever so many issues of martyrdom running rampant on your planet today. There are those who are martyrs for the "'Thou shalt nots." How they want others to admire them as they suffer "without" things. Perhaps they have chosen poverty and spout religiosity from their poverty. "I might be poor financially," they plead, "but my heart is right with God and I know that He loves me." Yes, indeed, they are loved by God, but not because they have chosen to be poverty-stricken in the name of God. They are loved *in spite* of this error in thinking. This is not to be construed as a praise of money. The limitations money imposes are another subject entirely. This statement merely shows another aspect of limitation, which is self-limitation as a means of attempting to be worthy.

There are those who shun so-called vices of others in a double whammy, as one of your plane would call it. With one disdainful shake of their heads, they are judging and condemning others for their faults as well as placing themselves on a pedestal as an example of perfection. In the secret recesses of their hearts, whether they choose to accept it or not, a number of these martyrs would like to experience some things that others are experiencing . . . but far better it is to them to deny themselves so that they might place themselves above others in the form of judge and jury. For it is so important that they—and only they—know God's thoughts and feelings. *They* have a hot line to His brain.

Let me tell you truth. *All* have a hot line to God's brain, but only in the issue of oneself. This is so very important to remember. The only issue one need be interested in is how one hears His voice about *oneself.* The issues and messages brought forth are individualized. Yes, all are *one*, but different factions of the One, each one living out one's necessary plan. How can one dare to judge another? Perhaps one is a master, chosen to return in a manner of teaching another in ways that appear wrong. Wrong to whom? *Wrong to whom?*

By judging others, one is literally darkening one's own light. This, as in your scripture, is brought forth truthfully. For, you see, there is only one direction one might take, and ▶

that is toward the light. If one follows this always, there is not a way that one might be engrossed in someone else's darkness. That would be to take one's focus off the light. If one follows only the light, one will not take a moment's glance at someone else's darkness, for one then would be veering off of one's own path.

Martyrdom . . . takes on many forms and disguises. The humble servant . . . yes, this service to others is so very admirable. It is to be revered, but only for the right reasons. Have you not seen those who dote on and serve others in the name of God and then administer guilt, pressuring those they've helped to join their church? Or those who use the time with others to tell them the error of their ways? This is not service! This is coercion. Yet they walk proudly, with their heads up, supposedly knowing that they are doing the work of the Lord. No, this is not so. They are doing the work of "me." In such a task as belittling another, they are thusly raising themselves above another. This is not truth. All are equal in the eyes of God.

True service is done in the name of kindness only. If one is willing to help another, asking nothing in return and taking nothing in return, then the true heart is in evidence. This martyrdom of helping is so many times used as a tool of manipulation. One might help another, and when this person will not help one in return, one might plead, "But I helped *you*. Look what I've done for you, and now you can't even lift a finger to help me!" Tell me truly, was the initial effort of helping the other person only for the sake of kindness? I think not. It was an instant IOU, given to the other person without that person's knowledge. This form of giving is martyrdom and manipulation—control.

With this in mind, think within how many true givers there are. They are few. But there are a great many debtors, ▶

all too willing to call in their markers.

Parenthood is one of the greatest martyrdoms upon your planet. Ah, yes. Parents dote on their children, providing for them, all the time doing without themselves so that they might be good parents. Ideals are embedded within the child's head to the degree that very few are given the opportunity to think for themselves. Their true voice within has been covered over with ultimatums from their parents. "You *will* go to college, for if you do not, you will be a bum. You *will not* wear your hair like that while in *my* house!" The list goes on and on. Then the time comes when the children are grown enough (or disgusted enough) to step out on their own—free at last to be who they truly are.

But who are they? It might take years upon years for them to discover this, for they are merely the molded thoughts and ideals of their parents. In experimenting with their thoughts and actions, they might choose not to attend college or become a doctor in their father's footsteps. What do the loving parents do then? They reinforce the message that the child is incompetent. "What do you mean, you're not going to college?!" they scream. "I suffered and scrimped and saved *all my life* so you could have this opportunity!" What a scenario.

This now becomes a triple whammy. Let us count: firstly, the reinforcement that the child's life is ruined if he follows his own issues; secondly, the child is responsible for ruining his parents' lives because their suffering was for nothing; thirdly, the idea is reinforced that he is ungrateful, stupid, incompetent and so on and so on, not to mention a major disappointment in his parents' eyes. How many times has a father said, "What do you *mean*, you're not taking over the family business?! I built this business for *you!*"

These same parents will go to their friends, clergy, whoever will listen, and tell their sad story of sacrifice. They did everything for this totally ungrateful child. They have not only placed themselves on the altar of sacrifice for their child, but they have also elicited sympathy and admiration from their peers. Martyrdom? In the greatest degree.

How many parents do you know who happily provide for their children, asking only that the children learn who they are and follow that path unending, with total support and unconditional love from them?

This brings us to the true core of this lesson. How does one break this pattern of martyrdom? With unconditional love. Only this strong and pure love will allow one to see others without the prerequisites one has placed upon them. One doesn't even ask that another love one in return. This should be a truly voluntary emotion, which in turn allows the other freedom to love one unconditionally. How might one expect another to love one in return to this great degree when regulations have been placed upon the relationship? Love, true love, is evident only when there is freedom.

Truly, the list goes on and on. Only when the people of the Earth have moved past this conditional love can they burst through the barrier of misperception into the light. The absence of martyrdom is the presence of God.

Regeneration

"Regeneration" was a prerequisite for my journey. Looking back I can see that had I not released the old, outdated me, I would have most certainly short-circuited as I went from one experience to another. This would have been a total loss. The new factions of me would have never been known, and the old ones would no longer function. I have to laugh as I envision myself how I could have been, possibly babbling incoherently. Regeneration is another element that is crucial to one's journey, regardless of the destination. This life is an adventure to be enjoyed.

Regeneration could thusly be called rejuvenation. They are the same. In this context it must be remembered that nothing remains the same. All is moving. All is traversing about to reclaim its identity. This might appear as a complex lesson, but as in the truth of all things, it is simple. Shall we begin?

Have you ever watched a leaf fall to the ground? It is both lovely and sad at the outset. One thinks of old life passing away to allow new life for the spring season. At the same time, one almost mourns the passing of life, of what was once alive and beautiful. This is with *all* things. The old must pass to allow for the new. This is regeneration.

For, you see, the tree goes on and on while it is here on Earth. Envision this tree as the spirit of you. The tree then sheds small parts of itself so that it may ever be new and beautiful. These small parts, the leaves, are much the same as when one being sheds the old pieces of *itself*. These small pieces or various factions have once been a part of one but must now be shed to allow for new factions. Let us look at the factions—or leaves—of oneself.

One might be the ideal that what you see upon Earth is all there is. As this ideal is shed, a new and brighter one arrives, ▶

which shows that there is much more. Have you not experienced many instances in which a glimpse of normally unseen reality is at your availability? Did you not need to shed old parameters of thinking to allow absorption of these facts?

Taking this to a more common, yet just as important aspect . . . perhaps one came into your plane with an ideal of selfishness or jealousy. This is apparent within a short time as the child develops relationships with others. Over time, events occur that mostly erase these ideals, which are then replaced with an attitude of generosity and love. Notice that I mentioned "mostly." Not all beings choose to release these backward emotions.

Now . . . thusly, what happens to a tree if it does not shed its leaves? Why, it would die, would it not? This, my one, is what happens to the spirit who refuses to release old and diseased emotions and actions. The spirit does not die into nonexistence (nor does the tree, for that matter, when it leaves the Earth plane), but it dies to the heart, the inner being of the individual. Notice those who have become hardened and cold. They are as if no life, "light life." lives there. This is an outward expression of the dying spirit. It is still there but no longer functioning, for it has been covered over and tarnished so heavily that it can no longer breathe. It has gone into what one might call hibernation until the "light of spring" (the light of one's thoughts and actions) calls it forth to blossom again.

Do you see how simple it is to understand the importance of regeneration? One must continually grow, shedding the factions—one by one—that are no longer needed for the trek home. "Aha!" you state. "This is where the term 'deadwood' is so appropriate!" And so it is. And so it is.

I sense a feeling of conflict within you in which you ask about a previous lesson. In that lesson it was taught that to change the outward actions, one must firstly know who one is ▶

and reunite with the light within. Now I state that one's actions cover the spirit. This rightly appears as a dichotomy. Let us look closer, shall we?

In the instance of those who appear cold and hard, it is indeed due to the fact that they have not touched the God within. In an instance such as this, many experiences or teachers might be placed in the path of these ones to assist in their growth. This is where free will has such an impact upon this process. These ones then have the *choice* to accept guidance and light, or they can choose to cling to the old and dead ways. When they make this choice, it is then *they* who are choosing to close off their God-essence. When this is done, the light will literally hibernate until the effort is made by one to regenerate it. Is this clearer now? Of certainty.

May your tree blossom continually with new and brilliant leaves. May you happily release all the deadwood and withered leaves.

Chivalry

This message was basically a summation of thoughts that I had been given in three previous lessons. Often my messengers would repeatedly bring forth the same ideas, with a different slant or from a different perspective. Over time I came to realize that the events I was experiencing were lessons also and, as with the verbal messages, some things became more obvious when presented in a different form.

Ah yes, my one. I note the complexity in your expression. Indeed, this appears as a strange subject for growth, does it not? Let us peer into this strange area and see how it ties in.

Chivalry is a word of old in your realm. At one time it was a description for an action that denoted gallantry, respect for another's welfare. Does it now become clear how it can relate to all in this "Now" time frame?

Notice how I use the term "respect" rather than "concern"? This is ever so important. Chivalry is all but gone in your realm, and it is a very important antidote to ever so many ailments, which are abundant.

Respect, in the form of chivalry, is taking into account another's value, responding to it in an elegant way. By doing this, one is not only giving respect to another, but also to oneself. There is also a form of respect that connotes awe which, in turn, births the effect that another is better than oneself. Do you see the difference? Chivalry . . . respect on *both* sides . . . ever so important.

With this in mind, let us continue, shall we? There is a time now, upon your realm, which is abundant in criticism of others, of blindness to others' divinity. Again and again I shall teach this lesson in various forms. Without seeing the divinity in others, it is impossible to reach one's *own* divinity successfully. That is to say that one is able to *realize* one's own divinity. It is always there, but the ability to see and realize it is diminished. ▶

If one is traversing along a highway and there is beautiful scenery all around, one is able to see it, realize it and take in its beauty, is one not? But what if this one erected billboards along this byway that stated over and over, "There is no beautiful scenery along this path"? One would not only be blinded from the scenery by the billboards, but one would also eventually begin to accept the message. This is what one literally does when one forms the thought in one's mind that others are lacking and not divine. This billboard in one's mind shadows and covers over the divinity of that other being.

Chivalry, then, is the ability to spiritually bow to others with the respect and admiration they are so deserving of, and it is also meeting them on *equal* ground. Let us take this a step further, shall we?

Suppose one sees *oneself* as less than divine, less than who one truly is? How is one going to see others if one is greeting them on equal ground? Why, of certainty, the other is also being greeted as less than divine. Also, supposing one, still seeing oneself as less than divine, perchance sees another as divine—what is this doing? As one greets another in respect (which now becomes awe), one is placing oneself *below* the individual one greets. This is not truth. This is not truth.

So then, how might one live only in truth? Only by seeing oneself and others in light. To do this, the act of chivalry must take place. See another as God-essence and respectfully acknowledge this one. Be willing to assist this one in many ways if needed, never losing sight of one's *own* God-essence . . . Chivalry.

This might be taken to level upon level in comparison understanding. Let us take a small peek at some examples, shall we? Pull forth the lesson on martyrdom. This taught that anything done when asking something in return is coercion and martyrdom. This is placing ones on different levels of ▶

value. At one time or another, *one* of them is owing the other, right? This is not chivalry. This is what you term "paybacks."

Let us look at the area of regeneration. If one does not see oneself as ever new, as ever the new creation, one is less than divine. Recall that chivalry requires respect of oneself as well as of another. Without the awareness of regeneration, this respect is lost within the trials. And *especially*, let us look at dominion. If there is awareness of divinity on *both* sides, there is no possible way that dominion or control can take place, is there?

This is why I say that chivalry is an antidote to ever so many ailments upon your plane. When viewed within this simple context, it becomes ever so simple, does it not [as in the lesson on simplicity]? As always, the pearls of wisdom are ever so simple if one sweeps away the deadwood and billboards that cover and hide truth. As humans, you have birthed the deadwood and erected the billboards; therefore, you have the power to remove them. Sweep away the clutter and let the *light* in.

Oil and Water
(Or . . . Remaining Balanced)

The message on remaining balanced was probably one of the greatest tools I needed to withstand the abnormal and sometimes bizarre occurrences that were propelled toward me, at times on a daily basis.

How does one go from breathless confrontations with extraterrestrials, Bigfoot, light anomalies and hissing five-foot reptiles to awaking and preparing breakfast the next morning, balancing the checkbook and chatting with others about the weather? I found myself disconnecting from the "norm." If the insurance agent would phone to discuss changes in the auto policy, I would think to myself, Who cares? I have little gray guys trespassing and you expect me to think auto insurance is important?

In reality it is important. This everyday life we are experiencing is crucial to our spiritual and psychological balance. If we begin to veer too far in either direction, we become off balance and dysfunctional in both aspects. We are living our lives here on Earth for a good reason. Yes, I gained much knowledge with the introduction to other worlds, but there is just as much knowledge to be gained in our human connections.

> My one, your heart is heavy because you do not know how to express your divine love to those around you. Divine love is of the spiritual realm, and you are living in—and dealing with—an earthly realm. This is to be learned.
>
> You are functioning in both the natural and spiritual realm, and this must be done, but it is a fine technique to be achieved in order to fully emerge into the combining of the two. Do not be disheartened. This is ever so natural for those emerging into the true spirit of their nature. That is connection to God. Be patient and kind with yourself
>
> Have you ever tried to mix oil and water? It cannot be done unless it is whipped together, and then it remains together for a short time only before it again separates. This, ▶

my one, is the equivalent of mixing the natural earthly things with the godly things. It is a delicate task, indeed. Only when the oil (spirit) and the water (Earth) are continually blended together can there be compatibility. One cannot step back and forth from one to another and remain grounded.

Take this as a recipe for your balance. *Continually* mix your earthly circumstances with spirit. Do not go from one to another. Blend them. Blend them. You continue to see yourself from time to time as the old earthly vessel. Your vessel is spirit, living in the earthly world. Once you can see this clearly, you can then pull the water into your oil. The oil has more substance, has it not? The water evaporates, does it not? It is temporal. As long as the oil is in close proximity to the water, they must be blended continually or there is permanent separation.

Chances

After receiving the following message, I thought, What is this supposed to mean?! I walked that land alone at night meeting God-knows-what, and now you're telling me not to be afraid of chances? I could have locked myself in the house, you know, and denied that those things were going on, but I *did* see it as something new and ventured out. I felt I wasn't given due credit for braving the unknown. I was missing the point.

I received the message on "Chances" after I had left the ranch. My messengers again suggested that I might consider sharing my lessons with others. I had been willing to share the experiences on the ranch in *Merging Dimensions* and now in *Dimensional Journey,* because I had photos to back up my claims. However, I mentally kicked my feet at the thought of sharing the messages because I could not prove they were real. Amazing! I had braved otherworldly beings and thought I had conquered fear, but I was still afraid to take the "chance" that I might be viewed as disreputable because of these messages or their source. I stalled for two years but eventually decided that the messages were not for me alone and how selfish it would be to harbor such information for myself merely because I was afraid of something "new."

"Chances" is a term that recollects thoughts of danger, of happenstance, of elements of mystery and perhaps fright. Well, with that one sentence, one would say, "I do not want anything of chances. All encompassed in it is negative." But this understanding is of an earthly perspective, so let us therefore look a little closer, shall we?

When infants are toddling, what would happen if they chose not to take a chance? Why, of certainty, they would be crawling until old age. Fear would keep them from stepping forth and becomming mobile. This is ever so elementary, and yet this is exactly what ever so many are doing at this time. They are "fearful" of taking chances. Let us look at these various chances.

▶

Perhaps one wants to step forth and assist others, and yet one fears rejection from another for one's insights. Or maybe one wishes to explore further one's abilities but has a fear of the unknown. Perhaps it is "wrong." No one *else* appears to be doing it. Perhaps one wishes with all one's heart to change one's life direction, yet the move would be so chancy. "What if I decide later that I don't like the change?"

Chances, chances, chances . . . let us remove this term, which has been so overused in a negative way. Let us phrase this instead as hidden opportunities, or perhaps "new"—yes, that is a very good term. So now let us look at these same instances in the context of the word "new," shall we?

One might say, "I wish to assist others, yet I fear rejection from others if I do something *new*." How limiting this sounds. Or, "I wish to explore more of my abilities, yet I fear this, for it will be *new*." Or, "I wish to change my life direction, but it would be so *new*."

Can one now see how debilitating it is to stop one's desires to grow simply because someone or oneself determines it to be a "chance"? If one is wise, one will eliminate this word completely from one's vocabulary. It is limiting and debilitating. What is the word "chance" implying? Why, of certainty, that there is a possibility of failure. If one believes the possibility for failure is there, one has already opened the door for that action to take place. It is saying that one is incomplete in one's divinity. One is saying that there are limitations for one's growth. Nonsense!

Again, let us look at any venturing forth as . . . "new" . . . new opportunities, new adventures, new loves, new visions, new *you* (as in rebirth).

Perhaps it is time to review many of the words in one's vocabulary to determine if one is allowing an old conditioning toward a word or the basic interpretation of that word to color ▶

or imprint within oneself a hidden barrier to growth, which is a limitation to the God-essence within. Remember, anything that denies the presence of God is unreality—how important one's words are and the implications or meanings that are encompassed within them. Is this not true?

This is merely another hidden source of tarnish or deadwood. Sweep it out now. Does one truly need anything telling one that one is less than a child of God? I think not.

So let us look at chances again. Chances, as in "new," are wonderful! Experiences, as in "new," are wonderful! Growth, as in "new," is wonderful! Begin, this moment, seeing your desires to step out as wonderful opportunities for the "new," and doubt *not one moment* that one is capable of accomplishing when one is capable of dreaming. Very simple indeed.

An Emerald in the Making

There were times when I chafed at the messages I received because I was either in error or veering off in a wrong direction and would bluntly, but lovingly, be told so. My buttons were pushed because I was told things I didn't want to hear.

On the other hand, there were times when I would lapse into sadness or a lack of self-worth, and the messages would lovingly and beautifully pull me up, brush me off, wipe away my tears and send me on my way with love. "An emerald in the making" was one of those messages.

Have you gotten immersed in unreality and lost sight of what is real? Let us explain. Have we not taught you that life is truly what you make it? Have we not shown that you, through your perception, create what you experience? Have you given your power over to circumstances that now hold you captive? It appears this is so. May we assist you in this dilemma?

You, our one, are capable and have the knowledge of seeing the folly in this, do you not? Yet it is often easy to lapse into backward thinking. First and foremost, your life there is your creation. If there is a lack, then you have brought it about.

Now let us look at perhaps your "perception," which is the screenwriter of your life. In truth, there is no lack if one is connected to God at all times. Yes, perhaps it appears as such when one has based one's life and needs on what is called the norm upon Earth. True value is based on the gems within, which are harvested and garnered through continual nourishment from the Creator. Have you a measuring rod for needs? Perhaps it could be measured as such. All upon Earth is temporal. It passes. The only everlasting thing of that plane is the love that binds spirit. This love emanates from God.

Let us look at gems, shall we? There are rubies, sapphires, garnets, diamonds, emeralds and so on. What you experience around you are the lesser gems. These are grand, and yet the greatest two are the diamond and the emerald, the emerald being the most cherished and valued within your monetary system upon Earth. The diamond is you, our one. Ever, ever so great, and yet still striving for greater value. An emerald in the making . . .

Now shall we compare these gems? All about you are lesser gems such as experiences, circumstances and such. These are trials at times, and yet they are still gems due to the fact that you are still growing as you experience. Using value as a measure, are you not, as a diamond, worth much more than the temporal circumstances you find yourself in? Most certainly! And are you not in the process of becoming the greatest gem of all?

What we bring to your awareness is this: You, as an emerald in the making, have surpassed the lesser gems that you are focusing on. You become what you see, what you perceive. Do not continue to give one more moment's thought to this lesser, temporal situation. To do so will block the evolvement of you as a completed gem. Is an emerald found surrounded by lesser gems? Nay! When an emerald is harvested from the Earth, there are *what* around it? More emeralds! The emerald finds itself surrounded with like gems. So you shall be. As you focus only on the emerald, the lesser gems will no longer be seen.

CHAPTER ELEVEN

A JUNCTION IN THE JOURNEY

In time, the messages started taking on a different slant. No longer were they elementary, providing only basic understanding of human principles. They now became more advanced, and the messengers explained to me that the information would entail guidelines for mastery. The following pages contain some of these messages.

Please do not assume that just because I received these messages I've graduated to a master. Far from it. I am still learning and often refer to these lessons as I experience the junction in my journey.

Mastery

When I received this first lesson on "mastery", I was still in the habit of reading book after book of enlightening material only to recognize that I already knew what the author was saying. In spite of this, I continued on with my nose in the books. Please understand that those books are provided for a very good reason. They (such as this book) are to assist others in their growth and, ultimately, their graduation into mastery. There comes a time when, as this message points out, we are to take the knowledge we've garnered and put it to use.

By continuing to relearn these things I was avoiding the next step in growth. We are assisted in this growth not only for our own benefit. It is for the benefit of all. As was stated in this message, as our light grows stronger we automatically assist others, which ultimately enhances and lifts us. We are all connected.

Mastery, my one, is a resulting factor that becomes one's whole being, whole essence. This is much like the God-essence within, except it permeates out until it encompasses one's whole being. It is much like a portion of yeast, which begins small, then overtakes all until all is expanded with it.

So, you see, mastery is merely allowing one's God-essence to become the driving factor of *all* in one's life. Very nice, is it not? Of certainty, it is, for this then allows one to experience one's divinity in all its greatness. Most upon your plane merely touch upon this essence, for mastery is not even an awareness for most, let alone a goal. But those who have an awareness of this capability for themselves can focus upon and bring about the goal.

This is where much of what you call magic comes in. Please do not bristle at this word. It is not used in the context of conjuring up spells, nor is it any form of witchcraft. Nay. This is not mysterious, nor is it uncommon. It is merely magical, mysterious and uncommon to those who are not ready for their "yeast" to activate.

There is a great difference between watching an event from the sidelines and participating in it. To watch is exciting, and one might cheer or boo. But when one is participating, one literally becomes "one" with the action. One *is* the action. This is much the same with mastery. To be somewhat aware of one's God-essence is grand indeed, for it allows one to open to more truth. This relates to many at this time. To do this, they read books upon books. They listen to others who spout enlightenment (and surely, many *are* enlightened), but what are these ones, who are reading and listening, doing? Why, ▶

they are watching from the sidelines! I repeat, this is grand. But as in a previous lesson, is it now time for some to lay down the teddy bears and approach a new birth? Of certainty it is. The time is so very short.

When one relies on literature rather than the inner voice, one is, at times, avoiding the next step, which is so very different and possibly scary. It is time. Do not watch . . . *be!* Do not stand there . . . *do!* To accomplish this awareness, one must allow oneself to shed the cloak of limitation. One must see oneself as, in truth, one is. This is a very big step upon your plane of monstrous limitation beliefs. Step forth, my ones, and experience what is your divine right. Perhaps this brings about thoughts of changing the physicality of something or being a magician. This is not what mastery truly means. It means that one has come to the realization that one is indeed a divine child of the God-essence and, as one's inheritance, one has at one's disposal the ability to create light in *all* one does and experiences. With the awareness of this abundance of light, one has then truly mastered all that might attempt to shadow one's light. As this awareness is brought about, it is the awareness that makes it truth in one's life.

In simplification, mastery is merely becoming *aware* of the truth of your being. One is no longer on the sidelines; one is participating in the event. One is writing and creating in light *all* factors of the life one is experiencing.

"But," you might say to me, "aren't we told that we already create what we experience?" This is truth, but the key word to mastery is *light*. If you reread what has been said, I have stated that the master creates *all* in light. Most upon your plane are creating with light and dark. The mastery is not yet accomplished to "see" how the dark is created within.

This is where all previous lessons to this point are tied in. One becomes aware of one's natural ability and the consequences of wrongful use. One then becomes aware of the generations and births within singular lifetimes. One then practices projection of thought to eventually eliminate dark covering of light, but the temptation is still there to flaunt this awareness over others. Once this temptation has been overcome and one no longer needs admiration or approval from others of one's ability to walk in light, one can then—and *only* then—step into the birth, joyous birth, of mastery.

Mastery II

Yes, my one, we have touched upon this subject ever so lightly, and there is so much more to be accomplished within this area, is there not? Let us begin.

Mastery is ever so complicated in most ones' thoughts and ideals and it has therefore seemed unobtainable to most. This is ever so much a tragedy. Yes, it was said that there are fewer masters upon your plane than most would assume, but it is equally important to say that there is coming a time when there will be ever so many. This will come about with the awakening. But to the forerunners, I add: Must one wait for the masses? Must one step aside and say, "I think I'll watch this other one for a time, and if all turns out okay, then I'll step through the door to mastery"? I think not. This is not for forerunners. One's accomplishments are meant to pave the way for others. One's growth is to be an example for others to learn from. This is much the same as an algebra teacher standing in front of a room full of students with blank faces, who know nothing of the subject, then stepping aside and saying, "Go ahead. Once you figure all this out, then maybe I'll be able to catch on also." Is this clearer now? All forerunners are teachers in one form or another . . . *all* forerunners.

Now that this has been clarified, let us continue. It is time to stand up, refocus on one's true position and begin functioning in that position. This position is what one agreed to do prior to arriving upon Earth. The time for stumbling and fumbling is growing ever so short. I may appear a bit harsher —or shall I say, intense—in this lesson than in most, but this is ever so important. Again, it does not mean that one must go out and take on the world or become famous in one's efforts. True mastery is thus: becoming a *continual* beacon of light for all to experience; continually knowing who one is and one's true inheritance; knowing at all times one's abilities as a child of Source; dropping all fear of the unknown and walking forth in certainty that all is as it should be and that as a master from *the One,* nothing will or can be wrong, for one knows that one will create all in light. Masters know that their being, their source, is first and foremost of all. In that context, how can anything other than Source have power over them? This is truth.

If one thinks back upon lessons prior to this, one can see that all that was given was a road sign to these revelations. This is a momentous time. This is the time for all cocoons to be shed. It is a calling forth of the troops of light.

Once one becomes *one* with this thought—again, *being,* not watching—then one can step forth and, in one's accomplishments, will indeed receive back ever so much more light than one is giving. This is universal law. It cannot be superseded. Therefore, one is at the controls for this measure of growth, as in everything else. Free will is flying in the face of most now, much as a flashing road sign. The arrow is pointing toward mastery and saying, "This way! This way!" And yet there is another path, which leads to the comfort of things known and already experienced. Which shall one take?

This lesson could be continued for many, many pages, but if this were to be done, it would merely be redundance. For, you see, as in all truth, it is really this simple. Why complicate what is simple? If one absorbs the few words in this lesson and carries them in one's heart, a volume of knowledge is encompassed within—or shall we say, it is the key to *open* the volumes of knowledge within.

Step forth, brilliant ones, and shed the costumes of ignorance, of everyday mediocrity. Within, deep within, one knows this as truth.

May your light shine always as a beacon toward home. May you be a lantern for those lost in the dark. May your paths lead others to God. May your blessings be abundant for all around. May you see yourself in this light.

EPILOGUE

MARCH 6, 2002

I occasionally have out-of-body experiences. Though I can always recall the feeling of leaving my body and returning to it, I usually cannot remember any details about my trip. This evening was different, though. When I came back, I was able to remember every single detail.

Just as I was dozing off to sleep, I felt and heard that very familiar intense whirring in my head. I knew I would be leaving. Inwardly I understood that I could refuse to go, but I willingly submitted and felt my lightbody leaving through the roof of our house. I recall wishing I was wearing something other than my almost sheer nightgown. "Perhaps," I thought, "someone there will have something I can put on over it."

Once I was outside I could see the stars above as I stretched my arms out in front of me and effortlessly allowed the energy to quickly sweep me up . . . and up. I could feel no cold on my body—even though this was Montana in March—but I found it interesting that I could see my breath. Two times I breathed out heavily, just to see this again. Soon I sensed that I was near an entrance of what seemed to be a ship; I relaxed entirely as I slipped inside and found myself on a walkway, which appeared to be comprised of a form of metal. The walls around me were of the same material, yet they had a grid-type pattern. I knew my way inside and happily walked forward.

Many people walked past me in the opposite direction, apparently leaving through the same doorway I had used to enter the ship. Most of them appeared to be distracted, with one exception: A woman stepped out of the line of people. She knew me and I knew her. This was a very loving, elderly woman of slight build, with short brown hair. We happily greeted each other, and then she quickly returned to the line of people exiting. I went forward, knowing exactly where to go.

Once inside, however, I found myself a bit confused. I was in an area that I knew was totally different than what I had been used to. I recalled that I had been here during other trips where I was lovingly greeted by humanlike people like myself. It was always a

homecoming. This time, however, the people appeared to be very unloving, and I sensed that there was a selfish nature to them; they were self-centered.

I then found myself outside, where the terrain was very harsh. The type of terrain I remembered was beautiful, and there had been many lovely dwellings, mostly reflecting a pristine white. In confusion I walked around, but no one appeared to notice me. After walking a bit further I saw a line of older, rundown, "mobile-home"-type dwellings. This, I thought, was strange; these were nothing like the dwellings I remembered from my previous visits, and I kept thinking how desolate it all was.

I walked over to some vegetation consisting of trees and brush. The branches were dry and brittle, and I found myself entangled in them for a moment. Then, out of the corner of my eye, I saw a man following me. He was somewhat heavyset, had light to medium brown hair, and he was wearing a scowl on his face. I felt uncomfortable and tried to hide from the man, but he was able to follow me to my hiding place. I yelled out for my angels.

The next thing I recall is sitting on a bench with three men beside me; one of them wore an orange-red stocking cap and was clothed in black, but I did not take notice of what the other two were wearing. At first I was alarmed, but then I recognized the man wearing the cap as one of my angels and laughed, pointing at the cap: "What are you wearing that for?!" The cap seemed very funny to me, and my angel laughed with me. I don't recall the exact words, but he responded along the lines of, "We needed to look like them." I immediately understood that my angels had saved me from that man, and in joking irreverence, I said, "It took you long enough to get here!"

My angels left, and I now heard a voice from someone I could not see. Automatically I sensed that the voice was coming from a godly presence. It told me, "You needed to see this and experience it. This is where one goes when one refuses to grow and change." The instant I heard those words, I felt myself returning, zooming back and reentering my body.

Upon returning from my journey and awakening from sleep, I remembered exactly what had happened and where I had been. I immediately left my bed to write down what I had seen and felt. This was unlike any of my other out-of-body experiences. Not only did I recall these latest events, but I also recognized the place where I had gone, suddenly remembering previous visits. After committing my experience to paper, I sat and thought deeply about what had just happened. Why was I told I needed to experience this? I believed I had grown and changed, and my messengers assured me that this was indeed true. Could it be because I was in the process of writing *Dimensional Journey* and they wanted me to relay this message? I could do that, but I wanted to leave out some details of my spiritual life that are sacred to me, that I didn't particularly wish to be scrutinized, debated and categorized within someone else's perspectives. As so often, the answer to my questions came from my messengers . . .

Our one, this was quite a journey, was it not? Most certainly. Let us look at your queries if we may. As you have deemed, this was not for your education. You have indeed grown and progressed to great degrees. This we have told you many times in many ways. But . . . as in your new book, you are a messenger to the people, are you not? This be so. You have been asked, if you may, to take this message to others. This is so very important. The time is coming when many will choose to leave your plane, but many also either hold to the arrogant myth that they no longer exist after exiting, or they assume that they will automatically progress to the "heaven" they imagine will be waiting for them.

As we have told you in times past, there are many levels of what is termed "heaven," and each is a separate dimension that accommodates the electromagnetic frequencies one vibrates to. Not all are prepared for the higher frequencies that abound in the realm many anticipate entering. This be so. This must be understood, and this lesson is given with the greatest divine love. It is not wished that any suffer or regret their choices while in your realm. Yes, there are many with ears that will not hear, those of a hardened heart; but there are others who do not clearly understand the progression of spirit after departure. As in a job one would apply for, there are requirements or abilities necessary for that position. As such, one would submit a resumé to present proof of one's talents. In this instance, one's heart is one's resumé, and the beautiful "heaven" is the job one is applying for.

Yes, we do understand your reluctance to "throw your pearls before swine." Indeed that is such a misnomer in the sense that humans are definitely not swine and this be understood. As you understand, it was termed such in an effort to state that one's sacred truths should not be defiled. This, again, is very understandable. Let us look closer, shall we? ▶

This is shown in the Bible as being stated by Jesus, is it not? What is portrayed throughout that text as his mission? Why, he threw his truths out there to assist those who had ears to hear. In the process, swine . . . those who could or would not hear, crucified him. This reluctance you feel comes from what? Fear! Most certainly, in your current day one would not be nailed to a cross, but there would be what one could term "verbal crucifixion." Yes, this is, indeed, a valid concern. Shall we look further at what Jesus accomplished? He enlightened many, many ones in his agreement to throw fear to the wind in the mission of alerting them to the fact that there was a better route. There was light abounding if they only would open their eyes and see, remove the blindfolds.

Would you, in a selfish way, keep this from others only for the sake of maintaining your dignity . . . or shall we say, keeping face before others? What would that make you? One of the selfish ones you visited on your trip. Aha! Please do not see this as a criticism of you in any way. This not be so. We bow to your courage and faith. We merely wish to shed light upon a perspective you currently have, which would prevent you from sharing this experience. Stand strong, go forth in truth and know that you are loved dearly. Many have much to gain, and you, our one, can assist in this. A bright shining star you are.

Linda Ball was introduced to anomalous activity at a very young age; her memories reach back to when she was just four or five years old. Like many other children of that age, she could see beings who the adults around her could not see, and she insisted that real learning came through the top of her head–not from her teachers in the classroom. Needless to say, she was told repeatedly that she had an over-active imagination, and her intuitiveness soon began to fade.

Linda had been working as a buyer of aeronautic equipment for a major government contract firm for several years when she began to experience phenomena again, in the form of channeled messages. Following her intuition, she abandoned her career and moved to Sedona, where she focused her energies on the spiritual aspect of her self. She soon moved to the Bradshaw Ranch, and her experiences escalated into breathtaking and inspiring encounters. In this book, Linda talks about the extraordinary phenoma she feels privileged to have experienced during her seven years on the ranch with rare frankness. She now resides in northwestern Montana.

Shamanic Secrets for Material Mastery
Speaks of Many Truths
Robert Shapiro

Shamanic Secrets—Robert Shapiro

Shamanic Secrets for Physical Mastery

COMING SOON

The purpose of this book is to allow you to understand the sacred nature of your own physical body and some of the magnificent gifts it offers you. When you work with your physical body in these new ways, you will discover not only its sacredness, but how it is compatible with Mother Earth, the animals, the plants, even the nearby planets, all of which you now recognize as being sacred in nature. It is important to feel the value of oneself physically before one can have any lasting physical impact on the world. The less you think of yourself physically, the less likely your physical impact on the world will be sustained by Mother Earth. If a physical energy does not feel good about itself, it will usually be resolved; other physical or spiritual energies will dissolve it because it is unnatural. The better you feel about your physical self when you do the work in the previous book as well as this one and the one to follow, the greater and more lasting will be the benevolent effect on your life, on the lives of those around you and ultimately on your planet and universe. SOFTCOVER 600P.

$19.95 ISBN 1-891824-29-5

Chapter Titles:

- **Cellular Clearing of Traumas, Unresolved Events**
- **Cellular Memory**
- **Identifying Your Body's Fear Message**
- **The Heart Heat Exercise**
- **Learn Hand Gestures**
  - **—Remove Self-Doubt**
  - **—Release Pain or Hate**
  - **—Clear the Adrenals or Kidneys**
  - **—Resolve Sexual Dysfunction**
- **Learning the Card Technique for Clarifying Body Message**
- **Seeing Life as a Gift**
- **Relationship of the Soul to Personality**
- **The New Generation of Children**
- **The Creator and Religions**
- **Food, Love & Addictions**
- **Communication of the Heart**
- **Dreams & Their Significance**
- **The Living Prayer/Good Life**
- **Life Force and Life Purpose**
- **Physical Mastery**
- **His Life/ Mandate for His Ancestors/ Importance of Animals/ Emissaries**
- **Physical Mastery**
- **Talking to Rain/ Bear Claw Story**
- **Disentanglement**
- **Grief Culture**
- **Closing Comments**

THE ANCIENT SECRET OF THE FLOWER OF LIFE
VOLUME 1

Once, all life in the universe knew the Flower of Life as the creation pattern, the geometrical design leading us into and out of physical existence. Then from a very high state of consciousness, we fell into darkness, the secret hidden for thousands of years, encoded in the cells of all life.

Now, we are rising from the darkness and a new dawn is streaming through the windows of perception. This book is one of those windows. Drunvalo Melchizedek presents in text and graphics the Flower of Life Workshop, illuminating the mysteries of how we came to be.

Sacred geometry is the form beneath our being and points to a divine order in our reality. We can follow that order from the invisible atom to the infinite stars, finding ourselves at each step. The information here is one path, but between the lines and drawings lie the feminine gems of intuitive understanding. You may see them sparkle around some of these provocative ideas:

- Remembering our ancient past
- The secret of the Flower unfolds
- The darker side of our present/past
- The geometries of the human body
- The significance of shape and structure

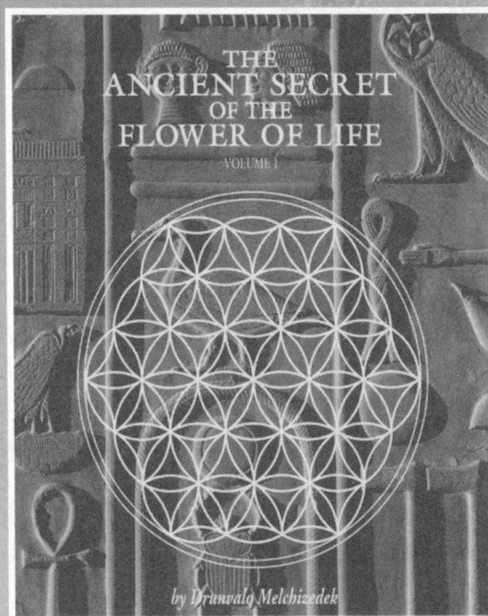

ISBN 1-891824-17-1
Soft cover, 228 p.

$25.00

Available from your favorite bookstore or:

LIGHT TECHNOLOGY PUBLISHING
P.O. Box 3540 • Flagstaff, AZ 86003
(928) 526-1345 • (800) 450-0985 • FAX (928) 714-1132
Or use our on-line bookstore:www.lighttechnology.com

Drunvalo Melchizedek's life experience reads like an encyclopedia of breakthroughs in human endeavor. He studied physics and art at the University of California at Berkeley, but he feels that his most important education came after college. In the last 25 years, he has studied with over 70 teachers from all belief systems and religious understandings.

For some time now, he has been bringing his vision to the world through the Flower of Life program and the Mer-Ka-Ba meditation. This teaching encompasses every area of human understanding, explores the development of mankind from ancient civilizations to the present time and offers clarity regarding the world's state of consciousness and what is needed for a smooth and easy transition into the 21st century.

THE ANCIENT SECRET OF THE FLOWER OF LIFE

VOLUME 2

ISBN 1-891824-17-1
Soft cover, 228 p.

$25.00

The sacred Flower of Life pattern, the primary geometric generator of all physical form, is explored in even more depth in this volume, the second half of the famed Flower of Life workshop. The proportions of the human body, the nuances of human consciousness, the sizes and distances of the stars, planets and moons, even the creations of humankind, are all shown to reflect their origins in this beautiful and divine image. Through an intricate and detailed geometrical mapping, Drunvalo Melchizedek shows how the seemingly simple design of the Flower of Life contains the genesis of our entire third-dimensional existence.

From the pyramids and mysteries of Egypt to the new race of Indigo children, Drunvalo presents the sacred geometries of the Reality and the subtle energies that shape our world. We are led through a divinely inspired labyrinth of science and stories, logic and coincidence, on a path of remembering where we come from and the wonder and magic of who we are.

Finally, for the first time in print, Drunvalo shares the instructions for the Mer-Ka-Ba meditation, step-by-step techniques for the re-creation of the energy field of the evolved human, which is the key to ascension and the next dimensional world. If done from love, this ancient process of breathing prana opens up for us a world of tantalizing possibility in this dimension, from protective powers to the healing of oneself, of others and even of the planet

- **THE UNFOLDING OF THE THIRD INFORMATIONAL SYSTEM**
  The Circles and Squares of Human Consciousness; Leonardo da Vinci's True Understanding of the Flower of Life; Exploring the Rooms of the Great Pyramid
- **WHISPERS FROM OUR ANCIENT HERITAGE**
  The Initiations of Egypt; the Mysteries of Resurrection; Interdimensional Conception; Ancient Mystery Schools; Egyptian Tantra, Sexual Energy and the Orgasm
- **UNVEILING THE MER-KA-BA MEDITATION**
  Chakras and the Human Energy System; Energy Fields around the Body; the Seventeen Breaths of the Mer-Ka-Ba Meditation; the Sacred Geometry of the Human Lightbody
- **USING YOUR MER-KA-BA**
  The Siddhis or Psychic Powers; Programming Your Mer-Ka-Ba; Healing from the Prana Sphere; Coincidence, Thought and Manifestation; Creating a Surrogate Mer-Ka-Ba
- **CONNECTING TO THE LEVELS OF SELF**
  Mother Earth and Your Inner Child; Life with Your Higher Self; How to Communicate with Everything; the Lessons of the Seven Angels
- **TWO COSMIC EXPERIMENTS**
  The Lucifer Experiment and the Creation of Duality; the 1972 Sirian Experiment and the Rebuilding of the Christ Consciousness Grid
- **WHAT WE MAY EXPECT IN THE FORTHCOMING DIMENSIONAL SHIFT**
  How to Prepare; Survival in the Fourth Dimension; the New Children

Available from your favorite bookstore or:

LIGHT TECHNOLOGY PUBLISHING
P.O. Box 3540
Flagstaff, AZ 86003
(928) 526-1345
(800) 450-0985
FAX (928) 714-1132
Or use our on-line bookstore:
www.lighttechnology.com

Behold a Pale Horse

Former U.S Naval Intelligence Briefing Team Member reveals information kept secret by our government since the 1940s. UFOs, the J.F.K. assassination, the Sinister Secret Government, the war on drugs and more by the world's leading expert on UFOs. SOFTCOVER 500P.

"I read while in Naval Intelligence that at least once a year, maybe more, two nuclear submarines meet beneath the polar icecap and mate together at an airlock.

"Representatives of the Soviet Union meet with the Policy Committee of the Bilderberg Group. The Russians are given the script for their next performance. Items on the agenda include the combined efforts in the secret space program governing Alternative 3.

"I now have in my possession official NASA photographs of a moon base in the crater Copernicus."

— Excerpt from pg. 94,
BEHOLD A PALE HORSE

$25.00 ISBN 0-929385-22-5

Chapter Titles:

- Silent Weapons for Quiet Wars
- Secret Societies and the New World Order
- Oath of Initiation of an Unidentified Sinister Secret Order
- Secret Treaty of Verona
- Goodbye USA, Hello New World Order
- H.R. 4079 and FEMA (Federal Emergency Management Agency)
- Anti-Drug Abuse Act of 1988 H.R. 5210, P.L. 100-690
- Are the Sheep Ready to Shear?
- Anatomy of an Alliance
- Lessons from Lithuania
- Coup de Grace
- The Sinister Secret Government
- Treason in High Places
- A Proposed Constitutional Model for the Newstates of America
- Protocols of the Elders of Zion
- The Story of Jonathan May
- Documentation: U.S. Army Intelligence Connection with Satanic Church
- Appendix A William Cooper's Military Service Record
- Appendix B UFOs and Area 51
- Appendix C Alien Implants
- Appendix D AIDS
- Appendix E New World Order
- Appendix F U.S. Government Drug Involvement
- Appendix G Kurzweil vs. Hopkins

Bill Cooper is a lucid, rational and powerful speaker whose intent is to inform and empower his audience. His presentation and information transcend partisan affiliations as he clearly addresses issues in a way that has a striking impact on listeners of all backgrounds and interests. He has spoken to many groups throughout the U.S. and has appeared regularly on many radio talk shows and on television.

LIGHT Technology PUBLISHING

LIGHT TECHNOLOGY PUBLISHING
P.O. BOX 3540 • FLAGSTAFF • AZ 86003
PHONE: (928) 526-1345 • 1-800-450-0985 • FAX: (928) 714-1132 • 1-800-393-7017

visit our online bookstore: www.lighttechnology.com

LIFE WITH A COSMOS CLEARANCE

Daniel M. Salter as told to Nancy Red Star

. . . IF THE GOVERNMENT DOES NOT COME FORWARD WITH THE TRUTH, THEN THE ALIENS WILL TAKE A MORE PUBLIC ROLE IN DISCLOSURE.

—Daniel M. Salter

On May 9, 2001, the Disclosure Project hosted a major event at the National Press Club in Washington, D.C. This historic event had witness testimony from twenty to twenty-five military, intelligence, government and corporate individuals, involved with UFO projects over the last fifty years, who presented their information before a worldwide group of media correspondents.

Those of us who were military witnesses of UFO history showed OFFICIAL GOVERNMENT DOCUMENTATION with our detailed testimony. Our focus was and is on the facts and documents. Our purpose was and is to get the mainstream media and government officials to hear those facts and move us toward an honest congressional inquiry.

We who came forward want to BAN WEAPONS FROM SPACE and stop aggressively shooting down these space vehicles and their extraterrestrial occupants. We need to declassify the advanced electromagnetic propulsion systems in use by the secret government, start producing them for the world to use and thereby help save this planet.

The people who had been employed in agencies within the military and knew THE TRUTH ABOUT UFOS had been sworn to secrecy. Now I am finally relieved to speak the truth. We military men who hold on to this knowledge are getting old and dying, and we want the truth to come out. We will either do it ourselves or leave it for our children and wives to do.

Personally, I have told those on Capitol Hill that I am being led to do it by the aliens themselves. They have convinced me that it is time. They have been waiting on the government, and if the government does not come forward with the truth, then the aliens will take a more public role in disclosure.

—Daniel M. Salter ISBN 1-891824-37-6 $19.95

Highlights Include

- The Kalahari Retrievals
- Weaponizing Space
- From Void to Mass: Wave Particlization
- Vienna and the Black Sun
- Germany's Advanced Technologies Prior to WWII
- The Brotherhood Lodges
- Secret Deep Underground Military Bases and Advanced Earth Craft
- Star Wars
- Russian UFO Files for Sale
- Approaching the Millennium Shift
- The Wingmakers and the Ancient Arrow Site

Agent Daniel M. Salter is a retired former counterintelligence agent for the Scientific and Technical Unit of Interplanetary Phenomena in Washington D.C.. He was a member of the Pilot Air Force, NRO (National Reconnaissance Office) and DCCCD (Development of Conscious Contact Citizenry Department) with the United States military. He was a CON-RAD courier for President Eisenhower, with a clearance far above Top Secret (Cosmos) and a member of the original Project Blue Book. His expertise was in radar and electronics, his field of investigation UFOs, Aliens and Particlization. Now seventy-five, Salter has both Comanche and French ancestry.

LIGHT Technology PUBLISHING

P.O. BOX 3540 • FLAGSTAFF • AZ 86003 PHONE: (928) 526-1345 1-800-450-0985
FAX: (928) 714-1132 1-800-393-7017 www.sedonajournal.com

visit our online bookstore: www.lighttechnology.com

$14.95
$9.50 CANADA
Peace to All Beings
SEDONA
Journal of EMERGENCE!
PREDICTIONS
BOOK
2004
AND YOU

Book 10 of the EXPLORER RACE

EARTH HISTORY AND LOST CIVILIZATIONS

by Robert Shapiro/Zoosh

SOON TO BE RELEASED

Zoosh reveals that our planet Earth did not originate in this solar system, but the water planet we live on was brought here from Sirius 65 million years ago. Anomalous archaeological finds and the various ET cultures who founded what we now call lost civilizations are explained with such storytelling skill by Speaks of Many Truths that you feel you were there. $14.95 Softcover

ISBN 1-891824-20-1

Chapter Titles:

- Lost Civilizations of Planet Earth in Sirius
- Ancient Artifacts Explained
- Ancient Visitors and Immortal Personalities
- Before and After Earth Was Moved to This Solar System from Sirius
- The Long Journey of Jehovah's Ship, from Orion to Sirius to Earth
- Jehovah Creates Human Beings
- Beings from the Future Academy
- Sumer
- Nazca Lines
- Easter Island
- Laetoli Footprints
- Egypt and Cats
- Three More Civilizations
- Medicine Wheels
- Stonehenge
- Carnac in Brittany
- Egypt
- China
- Tibet and Japan
- Siberia
- Natural Foods/Sacrament of Foods
- SSG's Time-Traveling Interference in Israel Imperils Middle East: How to Resolve It

ROBERT SHAPIRO

ZOOSH AND OTHERS THROUGH ROBERT SHAPIRO

Superchannel Robert Shapiro can communicate with any personality anywhere and anywhen. He has been a professional channel for over twenty-five years and channels with an exceptionally clear and profound connection.

visit our online bookstore: www.lighttechnology.com